THE

CANDLE

Poems of Our 20th Century Holocausts

Also by William Heyen

POETRY

Depth of Field (1970)

Noise in the Trees: Poems and a Memoir (1974)

The Swastika Poems (1977)

Long Island Light: Poems and a Memoir (1979)

The City Parables (1980)

Lord Dragonfly: Five Sequences (1981)

Erika: Poems of the Holocaust (1984)

The Chestnut Rain (1986)

Brockport, New York: Beginning with "And" (1988)

Pterodactyl Rose: Poems of Ecology (1991)

Ribbons: The Gulf War (1991)

The Host: Selected Poems 1965–1990 (1994)

Crazy Horse in Stillness (1996)

Diana, Charles, & the Queen (1998)

Shoah Train (2003)

The Rope (2003)

The Confessions of Doc Williams & Other Poems (2006)

To William Merwin: A Poem (2007)

A Poetics of Hiroshima (2008)

The Angel Voices (2010)

Straight's Suite for Craig Cotter & Frank O'Hara (2012)

The Football Corporations (2012)

Hiroshima Suite (2012)

Crazy Horse & the Custers (2015)

PROSE

Vic Holyfield & the Class of 1957: A Romance (1986)
With Me Far Away: A Memoir (1994)
Pig Notes & Dumb Music: Prose on Poetry (1998)
The Hummingbird Corporation: Stories (2003)
Home: Autobiographies, Etc. (2004)
Titanic & Iceberg: Early Essays & Reviews (2006)
The Cabin: Journal 1964–1984 (2012)
Hannelore: Journal 1984–1990 (2013)
Poker & Poets: Journal 1991–1995 (2015)

ANTHOLOGIES

A Profile of Theodore Roethke (Ed. 1971)
American Poets in 1976 (Ed. 1976)
The Generation of 2000: Contemporary American Poets (Ed. 1984)
Dumb Beautiful Ministers: Poets from the *Long Island Quarterly* (Ed. 1996)
September 11, 2001: American Writers Respond (Ed. 2002)

On William Heyen's Poetry

On *The Swastika Poems* (1977) and *Erika: Poems of the Holocaust* (1984):

"I lay the book down, heartsick, with a scream rising to my lips of the horse dying in the Picasso painting, *Guernica*. I have written many poems of the brutality of man to man, but not one has been able to cleanse me of the blood of those crimes, and now *The Swastika Poems*. What is there to say? I bow my head, sickened, until death takes me."

David Ignatow

"A surprisingly powerful work—surprising because we think of the Nazi attempt to extermi-nate the Jews as a horror which has now receded into a nightmare past. Heyen, because he is truly a poet, knows better—knows that it is a horror which will renew itself over and over as long as human beings ask the inescapable question: *What is man?* For it is this question which haunts these poems. Heyen is himself an American. But he is an American who is the son of Germans of the generation which produced the Nazis, and the nephew of a Nazi flyer shot down over Russia, and the question, *What is man?*, becomes for him the more agoniz-ing question, *What am I?* This question only poetry can answer—and poetry only when it is written with discipline and honesty and courage and restraint. As this book is written."

Archibald MacLeish

"The most powerful book I have read this year is William Heyen's *The Swastika Poems* . . . . I know no other book so firmly integrated . . . . Sober and chilling, songs in shadowed mea-sures, each leading forward into intenser realizations, darker clarities, these poems will invade your dreams."

Hayden Carruth in *The Nation*

"William Heyen's *The Swastika Poems* is a fine and large achievement. It's the book of one 'Born in Brooklyn of German parents,' who feels that he must confront the Nazi murder of the Jews, and discover both how far he is attached to his heritage and how far he must repudiate it. His personal enquiry, which is genuine, subtle, and never sensational, ultimately broadens . . . to include us all . . . . Much of the book's force comes of its being, in the most unforced way, a single poem of sustained strength."

Richard Wilbur

"For me, after two years of interviews with former Nazi doctors and Auschwitz survivors, *The Swastika Poems* was healing in a way I found nothing less than exhilarating, . . . and I have not had a similar sense of artistic transcendence since the film *Night and Fog*."

Robert Jay Lifton

"*The Swastika Poems* is perhaps the best book of poems by an American poet in this decade. It will be remembered long after more popular, undeservedly praised books have been long forgotten."

Martin Grossman in *Skywriting*

"Heyen's book, in particular, announced that American poets could write authentic and powerful poems about the Holocaust by reaching deeply within themselves, by opening the wounds of their true identities as children of the post-Holocaust world. His need, his daring, pointed the way. And others have followed."

Charles Fishman in *Poetry Pilot*

"As 20th-century poetry that is nakedly quintessential, William Heyen's *Erika* poems are unmatched. For it is a staggering paradox that the poetry of the Holocaust is best written by non-Jews. Written by Jews the poems of the Holocaust add to the literature of lamentation, the basic literature of the Old Testament. No matter how hauntingly great such works may be they cannot escape self-identification and the voice of the dirge. But to treat the Holocaust in a larger context, to throw light on the poetry of the victim one must be otherwise than the victim. One must be able to write a poem like "Riddle" or dozens of other of Heyen's *Erika* poems. Heyen has the added advantage, too, of being of German origin, some of whose family were themselves Nazis. This is the poet with the 'right credentials.' And this is where the true Holocaust poems come from. I doubt if they can be equaled."

Karl Shapiro

[*Erika* is] "an act of strenuous self witness . . . about the function of the imagination—its power and its limits when it comes up against the presumably untransformable facts of the Holocaust . . . as in the incredibly powerful "Poem Touching the Gestapo" or "The Trains.""

Jorie Graham in *New York Times Book Review*

"The poems succeed because they manage completely to free themselves of the maudlin, the sentimental-cum-sensational guilt-horror, the posturings, vanities and easy penitential gestures that the subject could invite. He has saved himself by arduous artistic integrity."

Anthony Hecht

"*Erika* is the flower that covers the area known as Bergen-Belsen. Heyen, a child of the WWII era, has the eye of Heine and the spirit of Paul Celan. His empathy is as total as if he were himself a survivor. This book should be required reading in every classroom."

Hans Juergensen in *Choice*

"In this bleak and searching book we find all Heyen's poetic preoccupations transfigured in a radically different perspective. In 'To the Onlookers' the Germans are addressed as 'you/ who could have been changed/into light,' suggesting both the deep mystical heritage of the people, and the likelihood that dissenters would have been burned in the ovens also. In 'The Trench' the enemy soldier to be   killed is 'the first black shape to fill trenchlight.'. . . The

Nazi consciousness is imagination turned inside out, exploited into evil. Heyen's translation of Celan's 'Death Fugue' is the best version in English, partly because he has found American equivalents for the very rich German and Biblical textures of the original . . . . *Erika*—the title is the name of a small blue flower at Belsen—is a book of obsessive dreams. The two words that come to mind when I think of Heyen's poetry are compassion and courage, and those qualities are nowhere more in evidence than in this volume. These are poems we must have and keep, spoken out of sadness and love."

Robert Morgan in Parnassus

On *Ribbons: The Gulf War* (1991):

"In this past year of 'our first war in the desert' and the 'amnesiac parades' which numbed our national conscience, William Heyen kept writing how the war hurt. Far from what used to be called the front lines, himself torn with Marianne Moore's old knowledge that 'there never was a war that was / not inward,' William Heyen stood watch for us all. These dark and brilliant *Ribbons* are, taken whole, the most self-demanding war poem of our century's death-throes."

Philip Booth

"Heyen deconstructs Operation Desert Storm to expose the perverse irony of terms like 'smart weapons' and 'surgically clean' air strikes. And he illustrates what he sees as the two-faced nature of American involvement (a war about oil masquerading as a war against tyranny) and the 'amnesiac' response of his fellow citizens. It is difficult to swim against a rush of sentimental patriotism and harder still to write convincing poems about such matters. Heyen accomplishes both, often with compelling insight."

Gardner McFall in New York Times Book Review

On *Falling from Heaven* (with Louis Daniel Brodsky, 1991):

"*Falling from Heaven* is a painful and poignant offering which reminds me that none of us has survived the Holocaust without scars. Yet, the distinguished work of the poets gives us the hope that maybe, if we are careful and courageous and alert and loving, maybe we can avoid a recurrence of such horror."

Maya Angelou

"What a powerful book *Falling from Heaven* is! Perhaps for the first time we see creation outside actual facts making its way through deep layers of the psyche as the Holocaust has done over the years."

May Sarton

On *The Host: Selected Poems 1965–1990* (1994):

"William Heyen's *The Host* is a strong, beautiful, important book by a poet in whom the 'visionary' and the unblinkingly 'historical' are dramatically meshed."

Joyce Carol Oates

On *Crazy Horse in Stillness* (1996):

"This is a special, powerful book. The old spirits don't bother with just anyone; usually, poets who try to invoke the indigenous spirits of the Americas fall short. With *Crazy Horse in Stillness*, it's as if the old spirits of the Great American Plains took possession of William Heyen and 'rode' his poetry on a journey of a thousand years into the past and into the future."

Leslie Marmon Silko

"How vital Heyen's poems are, and how rich and riveting the experience reading them through and then returning to begin again . . . . Heyen's book explores the various legacies of the Little Bighorn battle through an astonishing scope of poems . . . . Thus the book's conclusion returns, through image and language, to its beginning, while the poet spirals more deeply into his own commitment to both the page and to history . . . . Such formal variety, including moments of comic relief, prevents one from feeling assaulted by Heyen's intensity."

Elizabeth Dodd in *Tar River Poetry*

"Long before this new work, I recognized Heyen as our century's poet of memory and conscience. No reader of *Crazy Horse in Stillness* can fail to see how powerfully he keeps fulfilling that sacred mission."

Aaron Kramer

"A powerful book of poetry, showing that the imagining and reimagining still goes on."

Larry McMurtry

On *Diana, Charles, & the Queen* (1998):

"William Heyen has channeled the ribaldry many royal watchers have always imagined—sometimes with good reason to lurk beneath the surface of the heir apparent and his former wife's personal lives. The result is . . . a sequence of poems tracking their states of mind from the time of marriage to the point of the royal divorce. Completed before the divorce and contracted for publication before Diana's death, Heyen's irreverence never strays into malice, though it can get pretty giddy."

Publishers Weekly

On *The Rope* (2003):

"The urgency and authenticity of William Heyen's voice are unmistakable, and the plain directness with which he presents his sense of the beauty of existence and the menace that overhangs it, and our share in them both. He speaks for the conscience of our time, and for what in our days is worth caring for."

W. S. Merwin

On *Shoah Train* (2004):

"A master of the lyric sequence, William Heyen takes another unblinking look from scores of compelling angles at the Nazi attempt to annihilate the Jews and at the creative process that attempts to comprehend such brutality. Each of the 73 poems in this obsessive and moving collection focuses on the same inevitable and liberating truth: In darkness and light we will always be linked. And the light that this outstanding book provides shines into the ignorance and greed that darken our new century."

The National Book Awards finalist citation

On *A Poetics of Hiroshima* (2008):

"William Heyen's music and meditations continue to amaze. I've just now read and absorbed all the poems of *A Poetics of Hiroshima.* I am not ready to write anything about them, except to express my awe."

Cynthia Ozick

"William Heyen's *A Poetics of Hiroshima* is in my opinion the best book of poetry written in the last decade."

Robert Gibbons in *Janus Head*

On *The Angel Voices* (2010):

"William Heyen . . . has written some of the most memorable fugues and mnemonics we have in English about the Shoah. After such heartbreaking elegies [*The Angel Voices*], what is next? One wonders how to go on and live in this knowledge, this music, this pain."

Ilya Kaminsky

On *Hiroshima Suite* (2012):

"*Hiroshima Suite* is as compelling and moving a sequence of poems on the subject of history, Time, poetry, memory, Hiroshima, the atomic age and so much more, as I have ever read in contemporary poetry."

Alan Botsford

THE
CANDLE

Poems of Our 20th Century Holocausts

WILLIAM HEYEN

etruscan press

Etruscan Press
Wilkes University
84 West South Street
Wilkes-Barre, PA 18766
(570) 408-4546

WILKES UNIVERSITY

www.etruscanpress.org
Published 2016 by Etruscan Press
Printed in the United States of America
Cover design by L. Elizabeth Powers
Cover painting: *The Art of Reading* by Samuel Bak
Image courtesy of Pucker Gallery—Private Collection
Interior design and typesetting by Susan Leonard
The text of this book is set in Garamond Premier.

First Edition

16 17 18 19 5 4 3 2 1

Library of Congress Cataloging-in-Publication Data

Names: Heyen, William, 1940– author.
Title: The candle : Holocaust poems 1970–2015 / William Heyen.
Description: First edition. | Wilkes-Barre, PA : Etruscan Press, [2016]
Identifiers: LCCN 2015046326 | ISBN 9780990322177 (softcover : acid-free paper)
Subjects: LCSH: Holocaust, Jewish (1939–1945)—Poetry.
Classification: LCC PS3558.E85 A6 2016 | DDC 811/.54—dc23
LC record available at http://lccn.loc.gov/2015046326

Please turn to the back of this book for a list of the sustaining funders of Etruscan Press.

This book is printed on recycled, acid-free paper.

Contents

"If you have not grasped it until now, it is time you did: Auschwitz signifies death—total, absolute death—of man and of mankind, of reason and of the heart, of language and of the senses. Auschwitz is the death of time, the end of creation; its mystery is doomed to stay whole, inviolate."

Elie Wiesel
A Jew Today

"The fear of the absolute Evil which permits of no escape knows that this is the end of dialectical evolutions and developments. It knows that modern politics revolves around a question which, strictly speaking, should never enter into politics, the question of all or nothing: of all, that is, a human society rich with infinite possibilities; or exactly nothing, that is, the end of mankind."

Hannah Arendt
"The Concentration Camp"

"The *tremendum* cannot be avoided; nor does it matter whether the non-Jew shares in the welter of the *tremendum* of the Jews, if only non-Jews regard *tremendum* as a configuration whose name is called in our language one event and in theirs another. Auschwitz or Hiroshima or Vietnam or Cambodia or Uganda—what does it matter as long as each person knows the *tremendum* that bears his name; and it is one name only, for the rest what endures beyond the name and binds each human being in abjectness and torment to the other is that the configuration overlay, the *tremendum* of the Jews becomes the *tremendum* of the nations."

Arthur A. Cohen
*The Tremendum: A Theological Interpretation
of the Holocaust*

"We had to prevent any illumination from getting out so the Germans wouldn't find us. So, in the dark, except for one small candle, our voices spoke, seemingly unattached to our bodies."

Joe Rosenblum
Defy the Darkness

"In a different tone of voice and with sadness, Father remarked that soon there might be only poetry left, and no readers."

Samuel Bak
Painted in Words: A Memoir

from

The Swastika Poems

(1977)

I dreamed I had a lovely fatherland.
The sturdy oak
Grew tall there, and the violets gently swayed.
Then I awoke.

I dreamed a German kiss was on my brow,
And someone spoke
The German words: "I love you!" (How they rang!)
Then I awoke.

Heinrich Heine
Tr. Aaron Kramer

A Snapshot of My Father, 1928

His hick tie
flares out into the granular wind,
his thick kraut hair sprouts from under a cap you
wouldn't be caught dead in,

but he's smiling, he's
holding hard to the ship's rail,
and he won't let go because he's on his way now,
he's on his way to America,

a country he smelled
when the North Sea warmed to summer,
a country he saw when the story in a reader said
river, trees, land, money.

So he's eighteen, and somehow
he's on his way now. The Atlantic wind
blows his baggy trousers way out in front of him,
and he looks like famine,

this hayseed
with bad teeth, this carpenter
sporting a jacket patched at an elbow, this Dutchman
wearing a new life in his eyes.

But he doesn't know
what he looks like, or doesn't care,
but just cares to hold tight to the rail because
everything will be all right,

he's on his way now,
my father, for richer or poorer,
smiling for fifty years now because he's going to make it
to America.

For Wilhelm Heyen

(d. 1940, buried in Holland)

I
Battalions of bone crosses
(lines of a chaplain's gestures

in a pre-battle benediction)
and a still-living soldier

fronting them, staring
into my eyes, into the dark.

He moves his right arm.
This is, and was, certain in time.

II
The film shakes, then holds.
He chars at the edges, burns,

but the film moves. Holland
snows. Soldiers dig trenches,

stack shells, string
barbed wire with cans, plant

mines. Night falls. The wire
rattles. The mines flower.

III
Your grave is just, but rest,
my twenty-year-old uncle, rest.

I'll say you walked with soldiers,
killed, were killed. The Dutch

cut medals into your chest.
That book of love poems

my father said you pressed
out of your heart is also lost.

IV
Wilhelm, your face, a shadow
under your helmet

fades from the gray air
of newsreels. You did not hear

your nephew inherit your name.
I've seen you move your arm,

scythe, pendulum, sipped
from your hands cupped with blood.

For Hermann Heyen
(d.1941 over Russia)

My Nazi uncle, those letters begging you
to bail out over England and plead insanity—
you got my father's letters, didn't you,
but kept saying you'd land in London
with the rest of your squadron,
as soon as the war was over, . . .
but your Fuhrer needed you in Russia, didn't he,
and the few who bailed out there were met
by peasants with pitchforks and scythes,
weren't they? Anyway, your plane
blew up like a sun, your dust
bailed out all over . . . while I write verses
wondering how your Aryan romanticism
started, and when, if it did, it died.

Men in History

I

Keitel *still* expected the secret weaponry
of deliverance, and scheming Goering
even *now* angled for power.
Eva Braun, shadowy queen
of this black bower, resigned herself
to long hours of waiting
for cyanide, or one more night's love
no war would rob her of,

but over the Fuhrer's last days,
as Berlin crumbled above him
and a fine dust seemed
to cloud his bunkers, he moved
divisions of ghosts across maps,
and others around him
kept asking themselves
if this had become a dream.

Shriveled, insubstantial, unreal
even to himself, he walked
with an old peasant's stoop
in a uniform stained by food
dropped by his shaking hands.
Above him, his Reich's burnished eagle
lay in rubble, flew downward into flame.

II

But now it was mid-April,
his birthday, his fifty-sixth
year to heaven,
and since it was his last, and since
he knew, he left for the last time
his shelter and eventual tomb—
sixteen feet of concrete and six of earth—
for the Chancellery's upper rooms,

where walls peeled, drapes were down,
and paintings he'd insisted on
were long since packed away.
A hat lay in an easy chair,
old newspapers haunted the corridors.
This man shook hands, blustered,
passed out signed photographs of himself
framed in silver. Often nostalgia
floated him back twenty years until
his eyes brimmed with tears he quickly
wiped away with the back of his hand.

III
Then it was over.
He took his leave, wound
back down to his bunker
to finish the war,
to wait for God to open
the iron gate of the sun
for one more soldier soon
to die. This architect, this

messiah, this man in history
would die just once,
would flame just once into a darkness
far past our spit and curses.
As he said to Albert Speer:
"Believe me, it is easy for me
to end my life. A brief moment
and I'm freed of everything."

IV

Born in Brooklyn of German parents,
I remember lines scratched on our doors,
the crooked swastikas my father cursed
and painted over. And I remember
the *Volksfest* at Franklin Square
on Long Island every summer—
smoked eel, loaves of dark bread,
raffles, shooting galleries, beer halls,
bowling alleys, boys in *lederhosen*

flooded by an ocean of guttural German
they never learned, or learned to disavow.
I remember hourly parades under lindens,
the sad depths of the elders' eyes,
talk of the North Sea, the Rhine of Lorelei,
Köln's twin towers, the Black Forest, the mountains,
the Hamelin piper who led everyone's children to nowhere.
But I, too, was a child: all those years there was one word
I never heard, one name never mentioned.

Riddle

From Belsen a crate of gold teeth,
from Dachau a mountain of shoes,
from Auschwitz a skin lampshade.
Who killed the Jews?

Not I, cries the typist,
not I, cries the engineer,
not I, cries Adolf Eichmann,
not I, cries Albert Speer.

My friend Fritz Nova lost his father—
a petty official had to choose.
My friend Lou Abrahms lost his brother.
Who killed the Jews?

David Nova swallowed gas,
Hyman Abrahms was beaten and starved.
Some men signed their papers,
and some stood guard,

and some herded them in,
and some dropped pellets,
and some spread ashes,
and some hosed walls,

and some planted wheat,
and some poured steel,
and some cleared rails,
and some raised cattle.

Some smelled the smoke,
some just heard the news.
Were they Germans? Were they Nazis?
Were they human? Who killed the Jews?

Stars will remember gold,
sun remember shoes,
moon remember skin.
But who killed the Jews?

Passover: The Injections

Clouds pass over, endless, black fruit dripping
sap from the branches of lightning.

We lie down in the field, thousands of us,
never mind the rain. Soldiers come toward us,

groups of three or four. The wind opens their long coats.
Underneath, their uniforms are black. The beasts

bend over to the babies. The babies cry, for a little while.
"We are living in Biblical times," a woman says.

I Dream of Justice

In old Prussian law, three categories of thieves are specified: of gold, of horses, and of bees. . . . It may have been this clarification of natural law which stirred the mind of the nomad, rousing in him an inchoate perception of order and continuity.

Kay Boyle

I

You who are poor, take back your coins.
You who are Jews, take back your teeth.
You who are shorn, take back your hair.
You who were brave, you who collapsed in terror,
you who are dead, take back all the lost days of sunlight,
for I have hanged the thief of gold.

II

Farmers, back to your herds,
for the steel tanks they sired are lost,
cavalry vanished into the red wind,
submarines burst like lungs.
Take back your herds,
for I have hanged the thief of horses.

III

The thief of bees thought,
when your bees swarmed,
they had gathered for battle.
Take back your hives,
which bore him such bitter honey,
for I have hanged the thief of bees.

IV

I have awakened.
What is it I have come to?
Far outside this morning's window
horses graze their meadow,
and the bright air around the appletrees is strung
with golden necklaces of bees.

The Trench

This is Verdun,
horizon of barbed wires
lit with flares.
Shudder of mortar on both flanks, and now
down the dreamed line the repeated scream:
gas. My thick fingers,
my mask unstraps slowly and heavily from my pack,
a fumble of straps,
buckles, tubes.
I try to hold my breath,
and now the mask is on,
smells of leather and honeysuckle vomit.
Poison smoke
drifts into the trench,
settles. My neck
strains to hold up the mask.
I will.
Behind this pane of isinglass
I am ready,
my bayonet fixed for the first black shape
to fill trenchlight above me and fall.
I know that all my life one
German soldier has plunged toward me
over the bodies of the lost.
I am ready for him.
We are both wearing masks,
and only one of us will live.

Darkness

Thirty, fifty, eighty years later,
the books read, the testimonies all taken,
the films seen through the eye's black lens,
it's getting darker. The words
remember: Treblinka green,
Nordhausen red, Auschwitz blue,
Mauthausen orange, Belsen white—
colors considered before those places
named themselves.
Now, the camps—I lose them—
where are they? If it is true
that I've always loved him, if it is true
that nothing matters, if it is true
that I am jealous of them, the Nazis'
hooked crosses, the Jews' stripes,
darker: I lie on a table

in the Fuhrer's chambers, waiting.
They do not see me, this dream
begins again, film circles and burns
eighty, fifty, thirty years.
He touches my forehead,
darker. He speaks now, says, somehow,
lower, tells me to speak to the lower power,
for once, to say, come back, enter,
I was once alive. The air
swims with words, hair twines the words,
numbers along a wrist, along
a red brick shower. Darker.
To forgive them, killer and victim—
doctor, help me kill
the Goebbels children . . . .

Across the street, now, a cattlecar,
stalled. Skin lampshades darken
under varnish. Fragments.

Can I call him back? Millions still
call him back in deepest prayer,
but the light diffused as spray, past
Andromeda , in spiral
shadows. Darker, always
darker. *SS* death's head oval
hollow deadface hole for boot—
fragments, the heroes all dead
in the first five minutes. . . .

To enter this darkness, to dig
this chancellery garden to my own
remains, to watch
as his scrotum lacking one egg
and his face stare up at the sun,
to speak with that charred jaw,
carrying this with me, darker.
Under the answer, this love I have,
this lust to press these words—
he tells me *lower*, and the black breastbone
aches with it, the last black liquid
cupped in the eyesockets
smells of it, odor
of cyanide's bitter almond,
viscera smeared to the backbone
shines with it, for me to say it all,
my hands around his neck,
mouth to mouth, my lips
to kiss his eyes to sleep. We
will taste this history together,
my companion: take a deep breath.
Take it. Smell almond in the air.
The leader lives.

Erika

They were points of transit, they offered impressions whose essence could not be held steady, was always vanishing, and when I inquire what there is about them that cannot be stressed and found valuable, to give a firm position in the topography of my life, I keep on coming up against what keeps retreating from me, all those cities become blurs, and only one place, where I spent one day, remains constant.

Peter Weiss

Buchenwald: a beech wood, a soft word shining with sunlight falling through yellow leaves. A name, a place of terror. *Ravensbrück:* bridge of the ravens, a word out of the medieval gloom. *Dachau, Auschwitz:* words with no, so as far as I know, particular root meanings, but words that leave us confounded and inconsolable. And *Bergen-Belsen.* The name whines like a missile or jet engine. It is a name from which there is no escape. And it is impossible to imagine what happened at Belsen.

My earliest memories are of 1945. I was five. We lived in Woodhaven, on Long Island. My father worked in the shipyards, building against the Axis. I remember the green gate in front of our house and what the houses on our street looked like and how close together they were. I remember a trellis that leaned against one side of our garage. I remember, though I did not know what it was at that time, the persecution we suffered because we were Germans, the swastikas my father scraped from our windows or painted over when they appeared suddenly in the mornings on our steps or doors. 1945. At Belsen, as the trees began to leaf that spring, Jews and other dissidents were being murdered by the thousands. I remember the day in 1945 that Franklin Roosevelt died. I remember that day because my brother and I were getting ready to go to the movies when my mother came outside and said that the President had died and the movies were closed. And that day, because Roosevelt had died, down in his Berlin bunker Adolf Hitler was pounding his fist on a table and assuring himself that God had sent him a sign, that Roosevelt's death signified that the Third Reich would now rise from rubble. And that same day, children our age were being put to death at Belsen.

Belsen is forty miles north of Hannover, out of the way, and was meant to be. You are not likely to visit the place, but if you do, if you find the sign to *Gedenkstätte Bergen-Belsen* and find the place and park in the lot outside the grounds, you will walk under pines past a caretaker's apartment to which the central building, a square and simple affair of glass and stone, is attached. From the outside it looks like a small art gallery, perhaps, or a gymnasium. You will pause outside its glass doors to read a sign whose legend outlines the camp's history.

In 1940 Belsen, an already existing barracks, became a prisoner-of-war camp, Stalag 311. Russian captives were quartered there when a massive epidemic of spotted fever swept the camp. April of 1943 saw the establishment of so-called Detention Camp Bergen-Belsen; Jews began to be collected there. In March of 1944 people who were no longer able to work were transferred to Belsen from other camps. In October and November of 1944 eight thousand women arrived from Auschwitz-Birkenau. A month later, the latter camp's *SS* Commandant, Joseph Kramer, took charge at Belsen. The camp grew rapidly, apace with his ambition. Within a year after Kramer's arrival the camp grew from fifteen thousand to sixty thousand prisoners, many of whom came from camps too near the front.

Nine thousand were executed at Belsen during the first two weeks of April, 1945. In the middle of that April the British arrived to liberate the camp, but despite their best efforts conditions were such that an additional nine thousand died during the next two weeks. Eighteen thousand died during that April. While I was playing in the Woodhaven streets, six hundred people a day died at Belsen. The sign outside the memorial building concludes with the estimate that at least fifty thousand had been murdered at the camp. Anne Frank, who wrote that she needed only sunlight to hope, was one of them.

You are not likely to visit the place, but if you do, and if you are there in December, as I was, you will walk inside into a single big room. The room will be dark and cold. You will find no bones, hair, teeth, lampshades made of tattooed skin there, and for this you will be thankful. But you will see a map that locates what were German concentration camps and their surrounding cells and satellites. The map is a spiderweb of camps, stations, deployment centers. Then you will see the photographs that cover the stone walls, images you've seen so often before: the mummified bodies, the Lugers held against the temples of old men, the huge eyes, the common graves from which arms and legs sprout like mushrooms. But this time these photographs are of the very place where you are standing: this is a dimension you have not entered before.

In one photograph smoke rises from the center of the camp above the barbed wire and shacks and pines. In another, you will see only the backs of seven women who stand above their graves for a last few seconds of life as the photographer trips his shutter. These are young women who must not have been at the camp for long: their hair seems luxurious, and they are not thin. Their dresses seem to billow slightly behind them, their hair seems slightly blown back from a wind blowing toward the camera. Now, as the seven women stand there above that ditch, their hands bound behind their backs, they can see dozens of bodies below them, perhaps the bodies of their husbands and children. For a few seconds, as the photographer arranged his equipment or simply brought his camera into focus, the women may have glanced up at the sky. They may have spoken to one another. They must have prayed. A few seconds after they stood up in the light and air and wind for a last time, they fell forward into darkness. They are still falling.

On another wall in this room you will see blow-ups of newspaper descriptions of the conditions the British troops found here in the spring of 1945. They had to burn the place to the ground as quickly as possible because they feared an epidemic. Corpses were hanging out of windows. The dead had to be buried in a hurry. There was no time for more than cursory identification procedures. The machine of the camp had run down as the British advanced. Records were no doubt being destroyed, no doubt the German officers and guards were making their own plans, no doubt the murder of the last nine thousand they had time to murder those first two weeks in April was an inconvenience. This was Nazi *Kultur*.

You will walk outside past the mass graves. Each grave has a concrete marker: *Hier Ruhen 800 Tote April 1945; Hier Ruhen 1,000 Tote April 1945; Hier Ruhen 2,000 Tote April 1945*. The graves are banked at their bases by a band of about two feet of stone, and then the earth curves and slopes upward, rising as high as your head. The mounds are shaped something like loaves of bread, but squarer, flatter. You might say to yourself: *They are really here. I am at Belsen, and these are the graves of people who were murdered here. This is the camp at Belsen.*

You will see that the graves are covered, as is the whole area, with Erika. Erika, bell-heather, *heide*, a heath plant, wild and strong. When not in bloom Erika is green, a dark green. A poem by the German poet Hermann Löns, who died at Verdun, begins: *"Grün ist die Heide, / Die Heide ist grün."* In December, Belsen is green, a dark green. But in early fall, I am told, Erika blooms a reddish blue or bluish red, and then Belsen must be very beautiful, the sun perhaps occasionally breaking through the cloud cover, a warmer wind perhaps rustling the stiff blooming Erika over the graves, the *Heide's* billions of flowerlets veiling the open spaces in shifting mauves and orchids and blue-purple shadows. It must be very beautiful and very terrible at Belsen when each fall Erika blossoms. I do not think I will ever live a fall day when I do not think of this place. I will be driving to work, or opening a window, or playing cards with friends, or reading, and I will think of Erika blowing green or blooming violet-red over the dead at Belsen. And whenever I see a starling, or crow, I will remember the crows that stroke their black wings against the wind there.

Bergen-Belsen is not a big place, and it isn't old: what happened there happened shortly before mid-century. And it isn't a complicated place. It is very simple. At the edge of the camp there is a shaft of white marble. The words incised on it are simple and direct. Its fifth and sixth words are painted blood-red: Israel and the World *Shall Remember* Thirty Thousand Jews Exterminated in the Concentration Camp of Bergen-Belsen by the Hands of the Murderous Nazis." And further down on the stone: "Earth Conceal Not the Blood Shed on Thee!" Bergen-Belsen is a simple place, but it is more eloquent than the cathedral at Köln. It is a simple place, and it is easy to remember: there may be just a few days a year when the Erika is covered with snow, but in the early fall it blooms in the shades of lilac, the blossom of memory.

And I will always remember speaking to the caretaker there. He said that he still finds things. When spring breaks he tills the soil or replaces a brick along a walk or transplants a tree or rakes through the Erika and finds

a rusty spoon,
   or a tin cup,
or a fragment of bone,

or a strand of barbed wire,
   or a piece of rotten board,
or the casing of a bullet,

or the heel of a shoe,
   or a coin,
or a button,

or a bit of leather
   that crumbles to the touch,
or a pin,

or the twisted frames of someone's eyeglasses,
   or a key,
or a wedding band. . . .

The Baron's Tour

Gaze down at the Rhine.
I remember it red
with Roman blood.
We have always lived in this castle.

This is the room of trophies: griffin,
boar, bear, the long hair and leathery scalp
of a chinawoman, tattooed jewskin.
We have always lived in this castle.

At the base of this stair, a door
opens to the Fuhrer's chamber.
In its center stand
candelabras of eternal flames.

We have thought to leave here,
but the labyrinthine passages,
the sheer plunge to the river,
the stones that have come to caress us . . .

This is the hall once lined by hearts
impaled on pikes. These are the stair rails
of russian bone. This is the turret
where the books are burned.

Come, see where kings entered
the grained wood of the oak bed
where you will sleep tonight.
One said he'd dreamed

of his whole courtyard filled with heads
whose eyes mirrored fields
inside of fields forever. We have always
lived in this castle.

Blue

They were burning something. A lorry drew up at the pit and delivered its load—little children. Babies! Yes, I saw it—saw it with my own eyes . . . those children in flames . . . . I pinched my face. Was I still alive? Was I awake? I could not believe it . . . . Never shall I forget the little faces of the children, whose bodies I saw turned to wreaths of smoke beneath a silent blue sky.

Elie Wiesel

To witness, to
enter this
essence, this
silence, this
blue, color
of sky, wreaths
of smoke, bodies
of children blue
in their nets
of veins: a lorry
draws up at the pit
under the blue sky where
wreaths rise. These
are the children's bodies, this
our earth. Blue. A lorry
draws up at the pit
where children smolder. The sky
deepens into blue, its
meditation, a blue
flame, the children
smolder. Lord of blue,
blue chest and blue brain,
a lorry of murdered children
draws up at the pit. This
happened, this
happens, Your
sign, children
flaming in their rags, children
of bone-smolder, scroll
of wreaths on Your blue
bottomless sky, children
rising wreathed
to Your blue lips.

The Liberation Films

Seeing the films:
now we begin to know.

A bulldozer working the piles of dead together,
its treads hacking horizontal ladders

into this remorseless German dirt
that translates flesh into Erika and flowers:

now we begin to know.
Seeing the dozer's

curved blade curl
the dead like a flesh wave

as high as our heads
toward necessary pits;

seeing bodies white
with necessary lime;

seeing bodies fall
over the graves' edges;

seeing eyes staring at nothing,
bodies falling in slow motion;

seeing stick limbs falling in slow motion:
now we begin to know.

Seeing the dead roll and fall
as though flailing their last air,

without words, without sound,
without one syllable of their last prayers:

now we begin to know You, Lord,
now we begin to know.

The Spire

Wherever I am, I am not supposed to be here. I am above the street, above cobblestones shining the black shine of night and rain. It is cold, but in this dream I cannot feel the cold, and wherever I am, I know, I have been here a long time. Great dark shapes hang in the air behind me. Bells. A spire, a fretwork of porous red stone rises above me. Bodiless, I am in the belltower of the cathedral above the square at Freiburg. I have been here for centuries. I am breathing the air that flows around the still clappers of the bells. The square below is empty. I have lived in this air, I know, since before the spire.

Something is about to happen. A straining of ropes, chains. The bells' clappers begin to slam against cold iron. It is as though the bells are inside me, as though they are echoing deeply and mournfully the sounds for dead, dead.

It is winter here, a drizzle of sleet sifting through the dark red fretwork of the spire, through the sound of the bells. In the east, toward the forest, the horizon whitens with dawn. Lord, help me, I cry, and awaken.

A Visit to Belzec

I

In the east of Poland,
in the Lublin region
where fumes of Sobibor,
Maidenek, and Treblinka still
stain the air: smell the bodies
in the factories' smoke,
smell sweet gas in clover and grass.
This is Belzec
where the death compound's gate
proclaims in Hebrew,
"Welcome to the Jewish State."
This is *SS* humor.
curse them forever
in their black Valhalla.

II

   *"At 7:20 a.m. a train arrived from Lemberg with 45 wagons holding more
than 6,000 people. Of these, 1,450 were already dead on arrival. Behind the small
barbed-wire windows, children, young ones, frightened to death, women and men.
As the train drew in, 200 Ukrainians detailed for the task tore open the doors
and, laying about them with their leather whips, drove the Jews out of the cars.
Instructions boomed from a loudspeaker, ordering them to remove all clothing,
artificial limbs, and spectacles . . . .*
   *"They asked what was going to happen to them . . . . Most of them knew the
truth. The odor told them what their fate was to be. They walked up a small flight
of steps and into the death chambers, most of them without a word, thrust forward
by those behind them."*

III

Listener, you have walked
into the smoke-streaked mirror
of my dream, but I can't,
or won't, remember.
Did my jackboots gleam?
Did I fill out quotas?

Was it before, or after?
Did I close the doors,
or did I die?

I can still feel
iron and cold water on my fingers.
I remember running
along the bank of a river,
under trees with full summer
stars in their branches,
sky lit with flares,
the arcs of tracers,
the night air wet
with the sugary odors of leaves.
Dogs barked.
Were they mine?
Were they yours?
Was I running from,
or after?

IV

    "Inside the chambers SS men were crushing the people together. 'Fill them up well,' [Hauptsturmführer Christian] Wirth had ordered, '700 or 800 of them to every 270 square feet.' Now the doors were closed . . . .

    "The bodies were tossed out, blue, wet with sweat and urine, legs soiled with feces and menstrual blood. A couple of dozen workers checked the mouths of the dead, which they tore open with iron hooks. Other workers inspected anus and genital organs in search of money, diamonds, gold, dentists moved around hammering out gold teeth, bridges and crowns." . . .

V

Listener, all words are a dream.
You have wandered into mine.
Now, as workers rummage among corpses,
we will leave for our affairs.

This happened only once, but happened:
one Belzec morning, a boy in deathline
composed a poem, and spoke it.

The words seemed true, and saved him, for a time.
The guard's mouth fell open to wonder.

We have walked together
into the smoke-streaked
terror of Belzec,

but have walked away.
                              Now wind,
and the dawn sun,
                      lift our meeting

to where they lift the human haze

                          above that region's pines.

On an Archaic Torso of Apollo *(after Rilke)*

We cannot experience that storied head
in which Apollo's eyeballs ripened like apples. Yet
his torso glows, candelabra by
whose beams his gaze, though screwed back low,

still persists, still shines. Or else his breast's
curve would never blind you, nor his loins'
slight arcs smile toward center-god, where
sperm seems candled from under.

Or else this stone would squat short, mute, dis-
figured under the shoulders' translucent fall,
nor flimmer the black light of a beast's pelt, nor

break free of its own ideas
like a star. For here there is nothing nowhere
does not see you, charge you: You must change your life.

The Numinous

Our language has no term that can isolate distinctly and gather into one word the total numinous impression a thing may make on the mind.

                                                                    Rudolf Otto

We are walking a sidewalk
in a German city.
We are watching gray smoke
gutter along roofs
just as it must have
from other terrible chimneys.
We are walking our way
almost into a dream
only those with blue
numbers along their wrists
can truly imagine.

Now, just in front of us, something
bursts into the air.
For a few moments
our bodies echo fear.
Pigeons, we say,
only an explosion
of beautiful blue-gray pigeons.
Only pigeons that gather
over the buildings
and begin to circle.

We are walking again, counting
all the red poinsettias
between the windowpanes
and lace curtains.
It was only
a flock of pigeons:
we can still see them
circling over the block buildings,
a hundred hearts
beating in the air.
Beautiful blue-gray pigeons.
We will always remember.

The Uncertainty Principle

I

Lord, must this end in prayer, or
does the Lord enter secular words?
What is in the wind? Does the wind's
red trail ever end? What is certain?
By the time Jacob Bronowski walked
into the pond—is it Your pond?
is it our pond?—what had he learned?

II

Through a whole hour of film
I'd watched Bronowski's eyes:
his glasses flashed
as though his brain were bare to sunlight.

The camera swung past tables of skulls
gathered in Göttingen by Blumenbach
over a hundred years ago:
from these bowls of bone rose

a column of Nazi
science, calipers, iron
maggots, monographs
building ovens
to precise human specifications.

I'd listened to Bronowski's voice
following what Rilke, speaking
of Apollo's torso called
"allen seinen Randern,"
all its contours that broke open the atom
only to wonder, a tolerance, a
smiled estimate of error, a
limit to light to render, a
melting, a wavery withholding, what
Heisenberg won to, something like

Quine's "radical translation," language or
particle physics flying from
earth to the stars we will
worry forever.
                    Still,
Erwin Schrödinger spat on his black-
shirt assistant's boots.

III
We pass beneath the connected iron arch
that still insists *Arbeit Macht Frei*
to the sky at Auschwitz,
pass to where Bronowski stands
dressed in a suit of his ideas, wearing
a black tie, stands at the edge of the pond
here in Auschwitz into which, as he says,
the ashes of millions "had been flushed,"

pass to where he stands almost
in a dream of his ideas here at the edge
of this pond in Poland, stands as though
at the ditch of his own death, says
"It was arrogance, dogma, ignorance that did this,"
and walks into the pond. The sun

candles his face, birdsong
trills from somewhere behind him.
Bronowski walks toward us, toward
the camera into the pond, bends over,
kneels, cups water in his right hand,
cups in his hand the mud, the residue of ashes,
bows here in the pond at Auschwitz.

IV

               of this pond Lord
          of this pond of all ponds
               of silence these
            words from water this
                  mist's gray
              radiance these

first rays of the solar ovens'
undigested yellow gristle these
corridors catching sunlight these
weeds' twists these daily
shifts these clouds this
smoke drifting waters' surfaces these
sounds escape these
voices escape I can
almost hear I
cannot hear these
columns of shadows this
evening this

night now again wind
moaning past its pads'
curled edges past
its lilies' red-black
blooms its
only tongues

V

Bronowski knew that he would do this,
would walk toward the camera into the pond,
but we could not know that he would do it,
would stand in the shifting mud of the dead,
would help us to touch the watery lives of the dead,
would break the iron beat of our minds to a flutter,
a chance, would say, once and for all this
only truth that will not murder, as human
smoke rises into the blue air of Auschwitz,
would say that the atoms escape, the pond lives,
the mind's only border is this blur of tears.

Simple Truths

When a man has grown a body,
a body to carry with him
through nature for as long as he can,
when this body is taken from him
by other men and women who happen to be,
this time, in uniform,
then it is clear he has experienced
an act of barbarism,

and when a man has a wife,
a wife to love for as long as he lives,
when this wife is marked with a yellow star
and driven into a chamber she will never leave alive,
then this is murder, so much is clear,

and when a woman has hair,
when her hair is shorn and her scalp bleeds,
when a woman has children,
children to love for as long as she lives,
when her children are taken from her,
when a man and his wife and their children
are put to death in a chamber of gas,
or with pistols at close range, or are starved,
or beaten, or injected by the thousands,
or ripped apart, by the thousands, by the millions,

then it is clear that where we are
is civilized Europe, during the years
from nineteen-hundred and thirty-five
to nineteen-hundred and forty-five
after the death of Jesus, who spoke of a different order,
but whose father, who is our father,
if he is our father,
if we must speak of him as father,
watched, and witnessed, and knew . . .

and when we remember,
when we touch the skin of our own bodies,
when we open our eyes into dream or within
the morning shine of sunlight
and remember what was taken
from these men, from these women,
from these children gassed and starved
and beaten and thrown against walls
and made to walk the valley
of knives and icepicks and otherwise
exterminated in ways appearing to us almost
beyond even the maniacal human imagination,
then it is clear that this is the German Reich,
during approximately ten years of our lord's time,

and when we read a book of these things,
when we hear the names of the camps,
see films of the bulldozed dead
or one boy struck on the head
with a club in the hands
of a German doctor who will wait
some days for the boy's skull to knit, and will enter
the time in his ledger, and then
take up the club to strike the boy again,
and wait some weeks for the boy's skull to knit,
and enter the time in his ledger again,
and strike the boy again,
and so on, until the boy, who
at the end of the film of his life
can hardly stagger forward toward the doctor,
does die, and the doctor
enters exactly the time of the boy's death in his ledger,

when we read these things or see them,
then it is clear to us that this
happened, and within the lord's allowance, this
work of his minions, his deluded

vicious dumb German victims twisted
into the swastika shapes of trees struck by lightning,
on this his earth, if he is our father,
if we must speak of him in this way,
this presence above us, within us, this
mover, this first cause, this spirit, this
curse, this bloodstream and brain-current, this
unfathomable oceanic ignorance of ourselves, this
automatic electric Aryan swerve, this

fortune that you and I were not the victims, this
luck that you and I were not the murderers, this
sense that you and I are clean and understand, this
stupidity that gives him breath, gives him life
as we kill them all, as we killed them all.

The Swastika Poems

They appeared, overnight,
on our steps, like frost stars
on our windows, their strict
crooked arms pointing

this way and that, scare-
crows, skeletons, limbs
akimbo. My father
cursed in his other tongue

and scraped them off,
or painted them over.
My mother bit her lips.
This was all a wonder,

and is: how that sign
came to be a star flashing
above our house when I dreamed,
how the star's bone-white light

first ordered me to follow,
how the light began
like the oak's leaves in autumn
to yellow, how the star now

sometimes softens the whole sky
with its twelve sides,
how the pen moves with it,

how the heart beats with it,
how the eyes remember.

from

Erika

(1984)

"The supreme tragic event of modern times is the murder of the six million European Jews. In a time which has not lacked in tragedies, this event most merits that unenviable honor by reason of its magnitude, unity of theme, historical meaningfulness, and sheer opaqueness.... Ultimately, the only response is to continue to hold the event in mind, to remember it. This capacity to assume the burden of memory is not always practical. Sometimes remembering alleviates grief or guilt; sometimes it makes it worse. Often, it may not do any good to remember. But we may feel that it is right, or fitting, or proper. This moral function of remembering is something that cuts across the different worlds of knowledge, action and art."

Susan Sontag
Against Interpretation

Stories

I

A few hours before Heinrich,
my father's father, drowned in the North Sea
in nineteen-twenty at twenty-eight, he
walked outside his small home at Aurich

to pack his nets, spread on hedges to dry
in the German sun. My father, ten,
helped double, and double them again,
hand to hand, eye to blue eye

with his father who would soon be dead.
The horse-drawn wagon drew away. The fisherman
waved farewell to his wife and three sons.
My father, as he always did, tossed

an apple to the rider who, this morning,
backlit, rode silhouette against the sun.
Heinrich's shade dropped the apple, the fortune
in eel, fluke, and mackerel it meant to bring.

This simple world of signs went on. The wind-ripped
brine-tinged fields lay fallow, flounders
dozed at low tide under the stars
in the mud flats until, at daylight, speared

by children. The hollow, the shadow, the dead whine,
the wrack father twisting at anchor in my father's chest,
the North Sea's black shine, the North Wind's lost
song, the painful windfalls—these diminished, but that son

who planed thin the blades of his father's ash oars
and mounted them where they have pointed fifty years
into the wind above that house—arrow, weathervane—
would be no fisherman. Now, on their way down

to the same ancestral sea,
the luckier Aurich sons know that Heinrich's soul
lives in the wind, his only home,
in the seawind. This is one story.

II

I remember walking with my father
near the blue spruce that smoldered in shade,
hunched and crushed at an edge of wood,
but alive in the blocked Long Island light. He bent over

to tie the shoe I lifted to his knee.
I was so close, this once, that when
he looked up, I saw his left pupil widen,
fill with the blue-tipped green-black tree,

and swell with tears. When I dream of this,
I know, as I couldn't then, his two brothers
are just dead. I cup his tears
in my palm, as I didn't then, and the spruce

rises, from this water,
so blue, so light I am able to hold it
above us. The tree's perfect
form branches above us. This is another.

III

Wilhelm was killed in Holland,
Hermann over Russia. The North Sea's spawn
did not miss a rhythm when Berlin
burned to the ground.

What if the world is filled with stories?—
we hear only a few, live fewer,
and most that we live or hear
solve nothing, lead nowhere; but the spruce

appears again, rooted in dreamed tears,
yes, each branch, each needle
its own true story, yours,
mine, ours to tell.

Three Relations

I (Aachen, 1935)

He came to our city,
and the people were shouting and crying.
They hailed the Fuhrer
as the deliverer.
I was in the crowd, caught
in delirium, a moving box,
pushed forward.
Closer and closer he came
in the glistening black car
through a sea of heads.
The people almost touched him,
but I could not lift my arm.
And now he was opposite me,
and he gave me a look.
It was a look of death,
there was the chill of death in his white face.
I knew it, then:
he was the incarnation of death.
I felt it in my marrow.
All those who cried after him as their redeemer,
cried for death.
His look froze my heart,
and I raised my arm,
and I cried *heil*.

II (Released from Dachau, 1939)

... and then, after warnings
not to speak of what we'd seen,
we boarded the train . . . .

At last, it left the Munich station . . . .

In the compartment, we talked about our plans.
We couldn't sleep, although we were very tired . . . .
Vienna's houses emerged from fog . . . .

I went over to the toilet mirror,
adjusted my hat over my shorn hair . . . .

The train rolled in. I stepped down from the car.
There is my wife, pale and worn . . . .

At home, my little daughter clung to me and kissed me.
I felt afraid that I was in a dream,
I feel afraid that I am in a dream . . . .

III (Sachsenhausen, 1944)

The small stone house stands by itself,
thirty meters long, thirty meters wide,
five meters high. Two small windows
with heavy bars. A lawn in front,
and a wooden shack, where people undress,
to shower, they think.
They walk into the stone house.

Concrete floor and no furniture.
Maybe two hundred nozzles stick out.
The two windows and door lined with rubber.
It's a shower, all right, but gas comes out,
and twists their bodies into awful shapes.
Gas does not put them quietly to sleep.
Their flesh is torn with their own or others' teeth.

Their bodies were bluish red.
We dragged them out of the gas house
by hair and ears and feet
and threw them on a flat wagon.
Each wagon had room for seventy bodies.

We drove the load to the crematorium.
We stacked them at the entrance.
Flesh does not burn like wood—

it takes a long time to burn humans.
Burning seventy or eighty every day—
it's slow going.
There is always a fire in the ovens.
Day and night
a whitish smoke blows out of the chimney.

A New Bible

He told me his story, and today I have forgotten it, but it was certainly a sorrowful, cruel and moving story; because so are all our stories, hundreds of thousands of stories, all different and all full of a tragic, disturbing necessity. We tell them to each other in the evening, and they take place in Norway, Italy, Algeria, the Ukraine, and are simple and incomprehensible like the stories in the Bible. But are they not themselves stories of a new Bible?

Primo Levi

Evening. A lamp glows softly, gives off barely enough light to read by. You and I are children, reading a book by the light of this lamp . . . .

Our parents are getting ready for a party. They pass back and forth in front of us. The lamp shadows them against the walls . . . .

We are reading a story from a new Bible. We are as quiet as the shadows . . . .

In the story, a master orders the children to come to him. They leave their trains at a station where a clock is painted on false walls. It is always three o'clock. The master welcomes them. In two hours, at three o'clock, the children are ashes . . . .

There is no end to this book. It begins again, with other stories, after its last page. The lamp seems to concentrate its light on our book . . . .

In the yellow glow of the lamp on the pages of our story, we see other colors—mauves, rose. When we look up at the lampshade, we see erika blossoms through which the bulb shines . . . .

We turn the page. It is three o'clock. So many trains converge on the station, so many stories.

Nocturne: The Reichsführer at Stutthof

All night the current
buzzes and crackles
through the barbed wire
around his camp.
Commandant Himmler,
in his sandstone house—
white, clean, rectangular—
dreams back to the murmur
of childhood pines,
to the murmur of the sea.
When he awakens and hears the wire,
he says to himself, Heinrich,
sometimes, in this life
you have found and made,
you are so happy
your heart wants to burst.

The Car

He said he'd save
just enough Jews
to fill one car.

He said he'd drive
that car himself
through the cities.

Last stop: Berlin.
Citizens throng
to see the Jews

his mercy spared.
Berliners count:
one, two . . . three, four.

Each Jew he thinks he
or she will be
among the four.

The Hair: Jacob Korman's Story

Ten kilometers from Warsaw,
I arrived in Rembertow where
hundreds of Jews had lived
until the wheel turned: *Judenrein.*

You think they let themselves be taken?
They would not fill the trucks.
Men were shot trying to pull guns
from guards' hands,

and hands of dead women
clutched hair, hair of *SS* guards,
blood-patched hair everywhere,
a *velt mit hor*, a field of hair.

The Funnel: Speech to Jews at Treblinka
by Kurt Franz

Why try to run? Why take risks? No matter
how far you flee, you return
to Treblinka,

a funnel whose upper edges are the ends of the earth. You
are near the bottom. Others are already
falling, falling
fast,

will pass you soon. Do not run from your
responsibilities. The earth
will be purged
of Jews,

and Treblinka will become for you a world of joy.
I swear this on my honor
as an *SS*.

Dark in the Reich of the Blond

I had my papers, but I was running.
I had my proof, but I was running.
I had my trees of Aryan descent,
but I was running,

but I'd been dreaming,
and woke beneath a pile of corpses.
I was happy, hidden,
and I had my papers.

The moon shone down, but I was hiding.
The stars winked down, but I was hiding.
The sky had eyes, and they were open,
but I was hiding.

I am here now, where you are, too.
I live here now, where you will, too.
We two will wait here, quiet, still,
while the night forgets . . . .

Do you have your papers? Lie here quiet.
Let the eyes run down like rain, let
the bodies turn to grass as we wait here
with our papers. Lie here quiet.

Kotov

Ivan Ivanovitch Kotov, short of speech,
clarity drifting away to mindlessness—
Kotov of stutter and suddenly empty eyes—
only Kotov, in all Russia, of all those locked inside,
survived the *dushegubka*, the murder wagon,
the gas van. Only Kotov, pushed with his new bride
into the seatless seven-ton gray truck,
stood on that grated floor, and lived. Only Kotov,
pressed together with fifty others, would wake
in the ditch of dead, half buried, and crawl away—
he'd smelled gas, torn off one sleeve,

soaked it in his urine, covered nose and mouth,
lost consciousness, and lived, . . . waking
in a pit of bodies somewhere outside of Krasnodar.
His wife?—he could not find her.
Except for the dead, he was alone . . . .
He stood up, staggered and groped through fields
back to the city, where he hid until the end.
Only Kotov, saved by his own brain and urine, woke
from that wedding in the death van,
in Russia, in the time of that German invention,
the windowless seven-ton gray *dushegubka*.

The Trains

Signed by Franz Paul Stangl, Commandant,
there is in Berlin a document,
an order of transmittal from Treblinka:

248 freight cars of clothing,
400,000 gold watches,
25 freight cars of women's hair.

Some clothing was kept, some pulped for paper.
The finest watches were never melted down.
All the women's hair was used for mattresses, or dolls.

Would these words like to use some of that same paper?
One of those watches may pulse in your own wrist.
Does someone you know collect dolls, or sleep on human hair?

He is dead at last, Commandant Stangl of Treblinka,
but the camp's three syllables still sound like freight cars
straining around a curve, Treblinka,

Treblinka. Clothing, time in gold watches,
women's hair for mattresses and dolls' heads.
Treblinka. The trains from Treblinka.

To the Onlookers (after Sachs)

When our backs are turned,
when someone stares at us,
we feel them.
You who watched the killing, and did nothing,
still feel the eyes of those dead
on your bodies.

How many see you
as you pick a violet?
How many of the oak's branches twist
into hands begging for help?
How many memories congeal
in the sun's evening blood?

O the unsung cradlesongs
in the dove's nightcries—
so many would have loved
their own stars in the night skies,
but now only the old well
can do it for them.

You did not murder,
but looked on, you whose dust
could have been changed
into light.

The Legacy

I am alive.   Those Jews are dead.
I am living.   They are dead.
I think of them.   They are dead.
I think of them.   They are dead.
I think of one.   He wants to speak.
I think of him.   He makes a sound.
I hear his sound.   He moans.
I hear him moan.   He is dying.
I am alive.   He is dying.
I am living.   They are dying.
I think of them.   They are dead.
I think of one.   She is dead.
I think of her.   She makes a sound.
I hear her sound.   She makes an *r* sound.
I hear her sound.   She repeats the *r*.
I remember them.   They are dead.
I remember his moan.   He is dead.
I remember her *r*.   She is dead.
I remember them.   They make sounds.
I remember them.   They die.
I remember them.   They are making sounds.
I dream of them.   They sing.
I hear them sing.   They sing together.
I hear their song.   Their song is mine.
I smell of almond.   They smell of almond.
I die with them.   They live with me.
I leave to meet them.   They come to meet me.
I am dying.   They are living.
I am dying.   They are singing.
I am dead.   They are living.
I am alive.   They are dead.
I am dead.   They are dead.
I am dead.   They are dead.
I am dead.   They are dead.

The Angel Hour

As I chew my morning cereal,
I remember the camps,
how victims tried to live on infected water,
their own diminishing bodies,
their will to bear witness.

In my fantasy, God is retroactive,
gives them one hour each day free from fear.
They will call it "the angel hour."
They will each have a bowl of cereal,
wheat flakes with nuts and raisins and dates

drenched in milk. They will eat slowly
when even the *SS* must cower and whisper,
Die Engelstunde . . . .
In this way, I save so many,
as I chew my morning cereal.

Mandorla (after Celan)

In the almond—what dwells in the almond?
Absence.
It's absence dwells in the almond.
It dwells and it dwells.

In absence—who dwells there? The King.
There dwells the King, the King.
He dwells and He dwells.

      Jewish locks, you do not gray.

And your eye—where does your eye dwell?
Your eye dwells on the almond.
Your eye, it dwells on absence.
It dwells on the King.
This dwells and this dwells.

      Human locks, you do not gray.
      Empty almond, King's blue.

Death Fugue (after Celan)

Black milk of daybreak we drink it evenings
we drink it middays and mornings we drink it nights
we drink and we drink
we shovel a grave in the air where there's room for all
A man lives in the house he plays with serpents he writes
he writes when it darkens to Germany your golden hair Margarete
        he writes and he steps from the house and it blazes the stars
he whistles his pack to come forth
he whistles his Jews forth lets them shovel a grave in the earth
he commands us play for the dance

Black milk of daybreak we drink you nights
we drink you mornings and middays we drink you evenings
we drink and we drink
A man lives in the house and plays with serpents he writes
he writes when it darkens to Germany your golden hair Margarete
your ashen hair Shulamith we shovel a grave in the air
        where there's room for us all

He shouts slash deeper in earth you there you others sing and play
he grabs for the iron in his belt he swings his eyes are blue
slash deeper you with the spades you others play on for the dance

Black milk of daybreak we drink you nights
we drink you middays and mornings we drink you evenings
we drink and we drink
a man lives in the house your golden hair Margarete
your ashen hair Shulamith he plays with serpents

He shouts play sweeter to death death is a master from Germany
he shouts play darker the strings then rise as smoke into air
then you've a grave in the clouds where there's room for us all

Black milk of morning we drink you nights
we drink you middays death is a master from Germany
we drink you evenings and mornings we drink and we drink
death is an expert from Germany his eye is blue
he shoots you with bullets of lead he shoots you precisely
a man lives in the house your golden hair Margarete
he sets his pack on us he gifts us with graves in the air
he plays with serpents and dreams death is a master form Germany

your golden hair Margarete
your ashen hair Shulamith

Poem Touching the Gestapo

Behind the apparently iron front of Teutonic organization, there was a sort of willed chaos.

Edward Crankshaw

The system of administration [at Auschwitz] was completely without logic. It was stupefying to see how little the orders which followed one another had in common. This was only partly due to negligence.

Olga Lengyel

You now, you in the next century, and the next,
hear what you'll almost remember,
see into photos where he still stands, Himmler,
whose round and puffy face concealed visions,

cortege of the condemned winding toward Birkenau,
and how to preserve Jews' heads in hermetically sealed tins,

der Ritter, knight, *treuer Heinrich,*

visions of death's head returning in Reich's light,
the Aryan skull ascending the malformed skull of the beast,
the Jew, Gypsy, lunatic, Slav, syphilitic, homosexual,

ravens and wolves, the Blood Flag, composer Wagner
whose heart went out to frogs, who, like Martin Luther,
wanted to drive Jews "like mad dogs out of the land,"

Heydrich dead but given Lidice,
Mengele injecting dye into Jewish eyes—
Ist das die deutsche Kultur?—
this vomit at last this last
cleansing and an end to it,
if it is possible, if I will it now,

Lebensborn stud farms, *Rassenschande, Protocols
of the Elders of Zion, SS* dancing in nuns' clothes,

Otto Ohlendorf, who left his Berlin desk to command
Einsatzgruppe D and roam the East killing
one million undesirables in less than two years' time,

lamenting the mental strain on his men,
the stench of inadequate graves,
corpses that fouled themselves in the gas vans,

the graves rupturing, backs, backs of heads, limbs
above ground as they are here, if I will it now,

the day-in, day-out shootings of Jews, some attractive,
brave, even intelligent, but to be dealt with
in strict military order, not like at Treblinka where
gas chambers were too small, and converted gas vans' engines
sometimes wouldn't start, the thousands already
packed into the showers for history,
their hands up so more would fit, and smaller children
thrown in at the space left at the top,
and we knew they were all dead, said Hoess of Auschwitz,
when the screaming stopped,

Endlösung, Edelweiss, Lebensraum, Mussulmen, Cyklon B,

"and his large blue eyes like stars," as Goebbels wrote,
and the Fuhrer's films of conspirators on meathooks,

we cannot keep it all, an end to it,
visions of loyal Heinrich, what engineer Grabe saw at Dubno,
he and two postmen allowed to watch, the vans arriving,
a father holding his boy and pointing to that sky,
explaining something, when the SS shouted and counted off
twenty more or less and pushed them behind the earth mound,

Stahlhelm, Horst Wessel, Goering in a toga at *Karinhalle*,
redbeard Barbarossa rising,

that father and son, and the sister remembered by Grabe
as pointing to herself, slim girl with black hair,
and saying, "twenty-three years old,"
as Grabe behind the mound saw a tremendous grave,

the holy orders of the SS, Lorelei, the Reichstag fire,
Befehl ist Befehl, Anne Frank in Belsen, jackboots, Krupp,

bodies wedged together tightly on top of one another,
some still moving, lifting arms to show life,

the pit two-thirds full, maybe a thousand dead,
the German who did the shooting sitting at the edge,
his gun on his knees, and he's smoking a cigarette,
as more naked victims descend steps cut in the pit's clay,
clamber over the heads of those already dead there,
and lay themselves down. Grabe heard some speak
in low voice, . . . listen . . .
before the shooting, the twitching, the spurting blood,

competition for the highest extermination counts,
flesh sometimes splashed on field reports,
seldom time even to save skulls with perfect teeth
for perfect paperweights,

his will be done, and kill them, something deeper dying,
but kill them, cognac and nightmares but kill them,
Eichmann's "units," the visions, the trenches
angled with ditches to drain off the human fat,

the twins and dwarfs, the dissidents *aus Nacht und Nebel*,

Professor Dr. Hans Kramer of the University of Münster
who stood on a platform to channel new arrivals—
gas chamber, forced labor, gas chamber—and later,
in special action, saw live women and children thrown into pits
and soaked with gasoline and set on fire—
Kramer, a doctor, who kept a diary filled with
"excellent lunch: tomato soup, half a hen with
potatoes and red cabbage, sweets and marvelous vanilla ice,"
while trains kept coming, families with
photograph albums falling out of the cars, the books
of the camps and prisons, the albums imprinting the air,
as here, we close our eyes, and the rain falling from photos
onto the earth, dried in the sun and raining again,
no way to them now but this way, willed chaos,

visions deeper in time than even the graves of the murdered
daughter who tells us her age,
in the round face of the man with glasses and weak chin,
Himmler, *Geheime Staats Polizie*, twisting his snake ring,

as now the millions approach, these trucks arriving with more,
these trains arriving with more, from *Prinz Albrecht Strasse*,
from the mental strain on Ohlendorf's men,
from the ravine at Babi Yar, from the future,
from the pond at Auschwitz and the clouds of ash,
from numberless mass graves where Xian prayer and Kaddish
now slow into undersong, O Deutschland, my soul, this soil
resettled forever here, remembered, poem touching the Gestapo,
the families, the children, the visions,
                                    the visions . . .

My Holocaust Songs

I

Some split *SS* backbones with axes,
but who can praise them?
Some filed like sheep into the corridors of the swastika,
but who can blame them?
Some found smoke's way to the cosmos,
but who can see them?
Some rose earth's way to grass and pond-pads,
but who can know them?

II

Dead Jew goldpiece in German eye,
dead Jew shovel in German shed,
dead Jew book in German hand,
dead Jew hat on German head,
dead Jew violin in German ear,
dead Jew linen on German skin,
dead Jew blood in German vein,
dead Jew breath in German lung,
dead Jew love in German brain.

III

Break down again, songs, break down
into pure melody, wind's way,
history sung in leaves almost lost,
atoms of singing darkness, the meanings,
the wailing songs of the Holocaust,
themselves dying, returning with spring, the bleeding
notes, break down, break down again, my songs.

The Vapor

Events wound down to chaos.
Wanting to leave some trace,
Dietrich Bonhoeffer wrote his name
in his copy of Plutarch.
That book finds its way home,
his own life glowing from the Nazi dark.

When we touch the book of such a man,
when we hear his hymn,
"O faithful God prepare my grave,"
or his last spoken words, "This is the end,
but now I begin to live,"
we breathe the Erika vapor of those dead

who may come to comfort, and to bless
when next the runic lightning *SS*
slashes down. He tells us God is helpless
here in the world unless we share
His suffering, and thereby raise
all grief to holiness, to praise.

The murdered German pastor
who would have killed the Fuhrer
still send us letters from his cell.
Sometimes, all God's prison bulbs go black.
Dietrich mists and wipes his glasses, sits back,
remembers a word that lights another candle.

The Halo

A sister tells the story of Chicha at Auschwitz,
how Irma Grese, that *SS* aberration of beauty,
forced Chicha to hold two rocks high,
rocks she would die for if they fell . . . .

Where did the girl in bone-stretched skin find strength?
Her arms trembled together at elbows to hold steady.
God, keep her arms straight, our soul riveted to hers,
for this is the hour of good against evil . . . .

The camp dies into grayish dusk and blacker shadow.
We see a halo glowing around her shriveled body.
From then to now, Chicha pushes the rocks upward until
the torturer returns, says, "Put those rocks down."

The Children

I do not think we can save them.
I remember, within my dream, repeating
I do not think we can save them.
But our cars follow one another
over the cobblestones. Our dim
headlamps, yellow in fog, brush past,
at the center of a market square,
its cathedral's great arched doors.
I know, now, this is a city,
in Germany, two years
after the Crystal night. I think ahead
to the hospital, the children.
I do not think we can save them.

Inside this dream,
in a crystal dashboard vase,
one long-stemmed rose unfolds
strata of soft red light.
Its petals fall, tears, small
flames. I cup my palm to hold them,
and my palm fills to its brim,
will overflow.
Is this the secret, then? . . .
Now I must spill the petal light, and drive.

We are here, in front of the hospital,
our engines murmuring. Inside,
I carry a child under each arm,
down stairs, out to my car.
One's right eyeball hangs on his cheek
on threads of nerve and tendon,
but he stills smiles, and I love him.
The other has lost her chin—
I can see straight down her throat
to where her heart beats
black-red, black-red.
I do not think we can save them.

I am the last driver in this procession.
Many children huddle in my car.
We have left the city. Our lights
tunnel the fog beneath arches of linden,
toward Bremerhaven, toward

the western shore.
I do not think we can save them.
This time, at the thought, lights
whirl in my mirror, intense
fear, and the screams of sirens.
I begin to cry, for myself, for the children.
A voice in my dream says
this was the midnight you were born . . . .

Later, something brutal happened, of course,
but as to this life I had to, I woke,
and cannot, or will not, remember.
But the children, of course, were murdered,
their graves lost, their names lost,
even those two faces lost to me. Still,
this morning, inside the engine of my body,
for once, as I wept and breathed deep, relief,
waves of relief, as though the dreamed rose
would spill its petals forever.
I prayed thanks. For one night, at least,
I tried to save the children,
to keep them safe in my own body,
and knew I would again. Amen.

This Night

Which is our star this night?
Belsen is bathed in blue,
every footworn lane, every
strand of wire, pale blue.
The guards' bodies,
the prisoners' bodies—all
black and invisible. Only
their pale blue eyes
float above the lanes
or between the wires.
Or they are all dead,
and these are the blue eyes of those
haunted by what happened here . . . .

Which eyes are yours,
which mine? Even
blue-eyed crows
drift darkness overhead. Even
blue-eyed worms
sip dew from the weeping leaves
of black Erika
over the graves . . . .
But now, at once, every
eye, every blue light
closes. As we do.
For rest. For now.
Which was our star this night?

from

Falling from Heaven

(1991)

Children's Poem: This Village

Many orphans from the camps of Europe settled
in this village in Israel.
They studied in school, played, worked the orchards,

but even ten years after the *Shoah*,
they buried bread in hiding places
in their living quarters. Thus

this village thrived but suffered from mice
fattening on bread hidden under mattresses,
in cracks and holes,

beneath floorboards, behind walls,
for who could believe, day after day, there would be bread,
except the mice?—

these kept faith in the children, and waxed.
In this village, the ravenous dead still
gleam in mice eyes.

The Dead

A survivor, years later, allowed himself to wonder
where the dead were,
all those hanged from beams in their own barns,

or slaughtered against walls,

or herded to their own orchards, shot into ditches,
or starved in cattlecars to camps,
who screamed for God in the agony showers,

who burned their ways into graves in the empty sky . . . .

But then, at last, he saw one, one thin woman in a cloud
in a blue dress wisping away from her,
dress he'd bought her fifty years before.

"*There* you are," he said

"there," and "there," as others appeared from the west
in bursts of sunlight & cloud,
whole families of them, streets and villages of them,

cities of them, clothed in vapor, returned

by rails of sunlight, by sweeps of cloud, in carriages
of burnished cloud.
He kept waving, kept crying out,

"Here, here I am, *here*,"

but as for them, they sailed over his head, horizon
to horizon, for the rest of his life,
doing all they possibly could forming, eddying,

obeying the wind.

The Lice Boy of Belsen

Hanna tells of a boy infested with lice
eating their way under his skin,
into his eyelids, his bony chest black with them.

His parents dead, his brother and sister afraid
even to be near him, he begs for space
from one tier to the next.

No use. He is finished this morning,
his corpse a susurrus of fleas and lice.
Hanna says there are thousands of such cases.

This was January 1945, just months from liberation
from the ferocity of winter insects to which,
in whispers, he now testifies, the lice boy of Belsen.

Sonnet and Haiku:
Forms from the Reich University

I
"A junior doctor should ...
if possible, establish the origin,
date of birth,
and other particulars . . . .
After the killing of the Jew,
the head of whom
must not be damaged,
he separates the head
from the body and sends it
to the appointed place
in a specially prepared
and well-sealed
iron canister filled
with preservative." ...

II
Canister of words—
Judaism suspended
in formaldehyde.

Scripture: Himmler on Mercilessness

(to his *SS* at Poznan, Poland, 4 October 1943)

To speak it is one thing, to practice it another:
not merely imagine, but commit extinction,

commit it mercilessly

but remain decent: this has made us hard,
this glorious page in our history

that never shall be written . . . .

Should Germany need a tank ditch,
he shall have it, though ten thousand Russian women

perish from exhaustion . . . .

Mercilessness. To carry this through. Glorious.
Mercilessness. Glory. For Germany. We, the *SS*

risen into the power of mercilessness.

"Canada"

Across landscapes here now forever beyond innocence, the Jews in their sealed torahtrains. Hiding in luggage among cookware & clothes, these words of their lost languages: this little lucky hearth's cricket "beauty" (how beautiful the crimson sunset), this mouse "hope" curled in a cello among spools of wool (a blue sweater for Sarah by next winter), "tradition" tied in blackstringed phylactery cubes among prayer shawls & shrouds, this cockroach "dignity," this vein of coal gemlight "star," these ringworms "love" & "will," these trained vermin "courage" & "human," "honor" & "blame," god's burnished reichsmark "fate" (ashes to ashes), grapes from the vineyard "time," cheese stenchwedges of "spirit" & "faith," these dentures "choice" & "justice," these lead crystal compotes "story" & "poetry" (Aharon dreamed his mother/woke in her grave below the river) all these to the warehouse, "Canada," that power to steal/stain/dispense/ divide/weld/wed each word, each aesthetic to its opposite, trancefragments, cargoes of incoherence, rabbinical monocles of "vision" & "transcendence," this free & wild & incandescent history, human cattlefreightcar sounds vowelling across Europe with   all belongings, the Jews' exodus

up the chimneys.

The Apple

I

In Israel at that time just after the war,
we did not have much to eat,
so when, at the beach, I saw an apple bobbing in the waves,
glistening red, far out, but an apple for sure,
I swam for it.
I did reach the object,
and, as I'd thought, it was an apple.
I carried it to shore in my bosom,
thinking of its juice and firm flesh.
But, inside, it was rotten:
it had been thrown from a boat,
or a cloud, for good reason.
Were you to eat a bit of my survivor's heart
even the size of an apple seed,
it would poison you.

II

In Israel at that time just after the war,
we did not have much to eat,
so when, at the beach, I saw an apple bobbing in the waves,
glistening red, far out, but an apple for sure,
I swam for it.
I did reach the object,
but it was not an apple.
Unbelievable as this might be, it was an eye,
perhaps from an octopus, or a shark,
or a whale, but an eye,
translucid red, a watery gel,
its pupil black and unmistakable.
Perhaps this was the eye of the angel
of the camps. I cupped it in my hands.
I swallowed at least one mouthful, to see.

Coin

What was a Jewish child worth, summer, 1944,
when the Nazis halved the dosage of *Zyklon B*
from 12 boxes to 6 for each gassing?

When released, the gas rose, forcing the victims
in their death struggles to fight upward,
but gas filled every pocket of air, at last.

What was a Jewish child worth when the Nazis,
to save money, doubled the agony
by halving the gas? 5 marks per kilogram,

5.5 kilograms invested in every Auschwitz chamberload
of 1500 units. With the mark at 25 cents,
this meant $6.75 per 1500 units,

or 45/100 of a cent per person. Still,
this was too much: sometimes the rationed gas
ran out during the long queue of consumers,

so children were thrown alive into the furnaces.
In the summer of 1944 at Auschwitz, a Jewish child
was not worth ½¢ to the Reich

which struck this coin, floating freely hellward now
into that economy, this 25-mark piece,
one risked mark for each line, gas

for more than 60 children for each line,
if it please God &/or the Nazis in their mercy
to at least gas them before they are heaved

into the flames of the Thousand Year Reich.

The Secret

The survivor spoke. I began to hear.
Not her cattlecar four eternal days from Budapest,
the dead buried under luggage in one corner—
I'd heard this before.
Not the shorning, the aberrant showers,
the corpse stink of soup—
I'd heard this before.
Not the electrified barbed wire—
but as though her sentences
shorted themselves out,
phrases that buzzed & crackled
under her breastbone barracks. Not music,
the gaunt band playing the walking dead
off to slave labor,
back from slave labor—
I'd heard this before, or tried to. But
red streaks of voice across
an ionized atmosphere,
gassed Hungarian clawhair
& ribnails & tongues, a burst heart
breaking into static as she spoke,
into cancelling sparks, her now
never-ending speechlessness, never.

The Power

I signed my book   *Erika*   for a survivor
who told me her mother's name   Erika

the platform at Auschwitz   freightcar
steaming and stinking behind them they

shuffled in line   toward   the immaculate one
Josef Mengele   in white   who   this time

distracted in business with another *SS* officer doctor
almost let them by   together   but

motioned them back   divided daughter for work
Erika   for her grave in the air   I

looked up   to the survivor's daughter   who wore
a dress of wildflowers   Erika

with long black hair   here where
I hold the power   to let them leave freely   but

they must not trust me   not even
on the white page   where I could be   Mengele's

admirer   *you*   *to one side*   *you other*
join your ash mother   you

understand   I can't say but
Erika &   Erika's daughter they   walk away

though I could hold them   believe me   please
hurry   trust me I swear they

walk away   together   believe me I want them
to trust me   Jews   never

trust me I'll keep   talking   tell them
to keep walking   away   tell them   please

trust me   never   tell them
schnell   run   tell them   believe me   hurry...

The Candle

It would do me no good to travel to Auschwitz.
It would do the dead no good, nor anyone else any good.
It would do me no good to kneel there,
me nor anyone else alive or dead any good, any good at all.

I've heard that in one oven a votive candle
whispers its flame. When I close my eyes,
I can see and feel that candle, its pitch aura,
its tongues of pitch luminescence licking the oven's recesses.

A survivor, forty years later, crawled up into an oven and lay down.
What of his heart? Could it keep pumping its own pitch light
here where God's human darkness grew darkest?
Whoever you were, please grant me dispensation.

Rudolf Hess praised the efficiency of these ovens.
It would do me no good to travel to Auschwitz, to kneel or lie down.
It would do me or God or anyone else alive or dead,
or anyone else neither alive nor dead no good, no good at all.

The survivor did crawl back out of the oven.
He took his heart with him, didn't he not, it kept beating.
He left his heart in the oven, and it keeps beating, black-black,
black-black, the candle of the camps.

Eyes closed, staring up into this, eyebeams of pitch luminescence,
and the pulse of it, the heart, the candle—you and I,
haven't we not, have met him, the one who lay himself down there
where the Nazis had missed some, welcome, welcome home . . . .

We have spoken the candle heart of the camps.
It does the dead no good, nor us any good, doesn't it not,
but keeps, black-black, its watch of pitch light,
and will. Any good at all. Wouldn't we not? The candle.

from

Ribbons: The Gulf War

(1991)

2. (The Reich)

At first during Vietnam, I didn't know squat.
Wipe the gooks out, I said to my TV set,
which seemed to listen & disgorge body counts.
But I wised up fast, & marched, & wrote, but
nothing much good: naïve passion alone.

The best of those poems, maybe, was in *The Nation*,
"Good Money After Bad," about swelling troop deployments
to expand the operation & replace the poor dead expendables
leaving the jungle in body bags. "Coin of the realm,"
I called the drafted victims, & this was mild compared

to the "dogs" & "lumps of dirt" in that manual
& apogee of resistance, the "Essay on Civil Disobedience."
By the long time enough protesters' balls & breasts
clogged the war machine, there were 50,000 names
in the bank for that black marble mirror memorial in D.C.

But I was moving toward the Third Reich by then
by reason of family & reading & ambiguous dreams
in which I ran from Nazis, but with them,
slept in haystacks, but knifed them,
torched a synagogue, but died with Torah in my arms.

3. (Wings)

Dick Hugo once called me about nothing except
to say he'd gotten married, had had a lung cut out,
& would be okay. He was happy & in love & writing.
This was after the White House reception for poets,
where I'd seen him briefly, propped against a baby grand,
blitzed with champagne & history like the rest of us.
Later he wrote me that he'd had to get the hell out,
early—" too many angels there." Jimmy Carter showed up
at the last minute for Rosalynn's receiving line.
My wife & I were next to Simic. When Charlie answered
"New Hampshire," the President's eyes lit up—
the "Live Free or Die" state's primary used to matter—
but then dimmed again with the hostages in Tehran
who would cost him the next election.
Dave Smith, Ashbery, Gwendolyn Brooks, Ammons & Levine,
Stryk, Jim Dickey & Jim Wright, Hall & Swenson &

Rod McKeun was there, who had sold more books
than the other dozens of us together, & William Cohen,
the poetry-writing Senator from Maine; & maybe Gene
McCarthy, whose gnomic *Aardvark* book I'd read—
half Senate jester & one-third politician. Readings, &
Karl Shapiro said something rough & true for the papers,
& we all departed limbo to decompress
& figure out again what to do except trust
to good verses, as royalist Herrick said.
I wish we'd posed on a marble staircase for a photograph:
the angels die off
who for one day visited the powerless residence of power.
I remember being with Han, alone except for the lone
honor-guard Marine standing in shadow in a corner.
One of the smaller rooms, blue or green. Candlelight.
A tall empire bookcase filled with leather wings.

5. (The Indian Wars)

I have a boulder out back that I stare at.
Iraq has just hit Israel with six or eight Scuds.
When I'm in power & luck, it's not dark
inside the boulder, but a black silence
edging toward radiance: eternity & nothingness
conjoin for peace. Scuds are cancelled by Patriots,

& vice versa.... Back by the boulder I once found
a Seneca arrowhead: this was the western gate
of the five tribes of the Iroquois nation.
In Tel Aviv, gasmasks are packed like lunch.
Inside my television, sparrows whirl in mad patterns
staying alive like yesterday's news which,

as the master of Walden says, is always the same—
a royal wedding, or a war somewhere, or a sultan
suffering from gout, or missiles in the weeds like pike.
Another weapon is named "Shrike."
Missiles, like us, have been "thrown into being,"
the natural tragedy of righteous thinking,

& we are flying 2000 sorties a day into almost no resistance.
"A lot of our old men have become boys again,"
says General Schwarzkopf, Commander of Allied Forces:
for our pilots, there's an element of sandbox fun
to fly in & drop laser-directed ordinance
when there's only one flak-joker in a hundred-card deck.

"Schwarz" means black & "Kopf" means head in German.
Germany helped Iraq plan & build their chemical weapons.
Things go round & again go round says Wallace Stevens.
Across Brockport, allegorical ribbons are imposed on trees.
Iraqi television shows the revered warlord on his knees,
praying. He'll keep faith, we'll keep bombing him to heaven.

9. (Sorties)

I compare notes with neighbors: never before
so many sparrows at our feeders,
thousands waiting out the Brockport winter,
despite hawks. One silhouette didn't shift
when I walked beneath it & slapped its tree,

& last night, quick in the branches of sleep,
leaf-sparrows by thousands teased the predator
to no effect: it digested light in the boughs,
& would. By this time we'd flown 5000 sorties
in the Gulf & had lost only ten planes,

a chance in 500 for each pilot on each mission.
The Iraqi dictator swears to gas Jews, as did
his spiritual mentor, says an Israeli spokesman.
My sparrow understanding scatters at dawn
when a hawk powers through the leaves.

12. (The Circuit)

Readings in Casper, Riverton, Powell, & Gillette—
the Wyoming Poetry Circuit, 1978. Long drives,
sometimes out of range of radio, & missed signals cancelling
one reading somewhere, & snow, & a stuffed bull buffalo
in the Plains Indian Museum, & whiskey at Wild Bill Cody's bar,
& bicentennial pumpjacks rusting the red, white, & blue,
& a missile base in the distance past a herd of antelope,
& a Stetson in Shoshone thrown at his girlfriend by a drunk
in peace chains & khakis & an arm prosthesis from the Nam
which now, war in the Gulf one week old, staggers again,
a season of grief gone by, into every American town.

13. (Conventions)

"This might be an oxymoron," says (I swear) a Pentagon spokesman
beginning to whine, "but why can't we have a civilized war?"
Meaning, I suppose, that when an American airman
bombs your neighborhood, killing maybe a few dozen
& maiming maybe a hundred in body & maybe a thousand in mind,
& he's one of the few planes hit & he has to eject,
& after you've done the best you could to drag
victims out from under debris & you've washed the blood
out of your eyes as best you could & you've captured the bastard,
you should treat him according to the Geneva Conventions,
as gentleman prisoner of war, a name & rank & service number
who deserves a shower & clean clothes. You must not,
as I would, as you would, I swear, if such a technician
killed your wife & children, you must not drive steel
splinters into his eyes until they reach his civilized brain.

20. (Aktion)

During the fourth day of the Warsaw *Aktion*, July 25, 1942,
Jewish policemen & civilian helpers were rounding up
scores of victims for deportation to the dreaded east,
Treblinka. They'd formed a ring of truncheons around captives
& beat those who tried to push out.
Down the block, two lorries waited, two Nazi soldiers
leaning against them. Witness Janina Bauman says,
"they watched the round-up lazily, talking and laughing
in the bright sunshine of the mid-summer day."

During the third week of the Gulf War, February, 1991,
I pay my taxes & watch the news I've paid for.
The Warsaw *Aktion* took place from 8–4 daily,
but CNN is round-the-clock & our bombers have night vision.
Thousands of citizens were driven to the *Umschlagplatz*
for torahtrain passage to Jewish heaven.
Leaning back in my Brockport easy chair,
I am lazy with decaf & waiting for my money's worth,
maybe a tank battle, or fuel-bomb suicide mission.

23. (Home)

On the tenth of December, 1971,
I stepped outside the visitors' building at Bergen-Belsen
to walk among the mass graves. Overhead,
an occasional crow gusted across the overcast;
on the graves, restless low Erika parted & flattened
with streaks of wind, then
recomposed. That night I drafted

a memoir that carried an epigraph by Peter Weiss who said
that only one place, where he had spent
only one day—Auschwitz—stood firm
in the topography of his life.
At Belsen, underfoot, after so much flesh
melted away, the historical solidity
of bones. I was born in 1940

in America, have spent much of my life in only
two places, & in poetry,
but since that one afternoon have yearned, as you have, for a home
beyond this one, this cave
now so smoke-choked with greed & hate
that we won't be able, for long,
to live in it.

24. (The Frog)

Lao-Tzu says, "Compassionate toward yourself, you reconcile
all beings in the world." Kuwait's oil wells
are all "deep-mined," we're told,

&, if set afire, could darken a few growing seasons around
our delicately-calibrated earth.
Iraq & its "19th province"

provide a research lab for our new "smart weapons,"
& the Pentagon's procurement cup
runneth over, but

because my own brain is bleeding missiles & meadowlarks,
I'm draining a bloodbank of ecstatic poems:
Ghalib declares,

"The world is no more than the Beloved's single face;
in the desire of the One to know its own beauty,
we exist." A perfect circle back

to Emerson's Oversoul: thus, murder is suicide, we bomb ourselves,
& all in a desperate heart-doomed prayer for Oneness
& home. This is the sound of the frog

that leapt into Basho's pond & disappeared, but its green face
surfaces, & winks, in my own cup of tea. I taste
the Tigris & Euphrates in every sip.

29. (Gifts)

First day of the fifth week of the war.
"Desert Storm" there, winter storm here.
In Iraq, the removal of bodies & body parts
& fused lumps of unidentifiable remains
from what we call a command bunker
& what they call a civilian bomb shelter

& which was one or the other, or both.
In Brockport, snow outlines pastel ribbons
in my neighbors' trees along our streets
cleared by nightshift plows, & sanded
as we slept. In Baghdad, women in black
search & mourn among the blanketed dead

dragged out of their devastated haven.
Air raid sirens are still keening
while here the snow softens everything
in the fallen world. A White House spokesman
informs us that human life hasn't the "sanctity"
for their president that it does for mine,

& I don't want to live, sometimes—do you?
The blankets are not khaki, but civilian,
in rich colors & sacred Islamic designs.
All day across this country we'll open
cards & heart-shaped boxes of candy.
Happy Saint Valentine's.

35. (The Heart)

One mid-century Long Island afternoon
I biked over for some schoolyard basketball.
My older brother Werner & his friends, that melting-pot gang:
Tony Routi, the Blumbergs, Ernie Olsen, Prez, Riley & the rest.
Later, they were just hanging around, smoking, telling dirty jokes,
when one of them—I've blocked out who—mentioned a movie
playing in Smithtown, a war movie. He said you saw
a Japanese soldier cut the heart out of an American prisoner.
He said the prisoner was still alive, & tied to a stake,
& the Jap had a razor-sharp sword, & cut the heart right out
of the prisoner's chest, right through bone, & held it in his hands.

I am fifty now & have heard, I guess, almost everything.
I have read Krafft-Ebing, true stories of genitals in soup,
& have followed serial murders on television, have witnessed
secondhand such lurid torture & dismemberment
that I am almost shock- & compassion-immune. I have seen
an American president's head blown apart, bits
of his brain & skull sticking to his wife's pink skirt,
& have been to Bergen-Belsen where Anne Frank died.
But I was only ten that afternoon when
for the first time in my mind a human body was cut open,

its heart removed, & I could not breathe well or sleep well
for a long time, & this morning, watching television news,
I heard a young political science major, one Randall Alden,
being interviewed at the University of California at Irvine
about this war in the Gulf, which he was for 100 percent,
& if it were not concluded very soon, he urged bombing civilians
& deployment of U.S. tactical nuclear weapons, & for him
the Iraqi people were not people, & our oil economy
was his religion, & I lost hope, for I knew, then, what had become
of the American whose heart had been cut out.

38. (The Truth)

Across Brockport Village, a blight of orange & yellow ribbons
meant to remember our half-million participants
in "Operation Desert Storm," those who put their lives on line
to protect our country, as our president says.
Darkening ribbons encircle trees, telephone poles,
mailboxes, porch rails—so I was understandably half bored
& half nuts with war & ugliness, so climbed to my roof
& tied a large black configuration of bow & ribbons
to my aerial. Up there, I saw how it divides the winter sky
with its alphabet of one emotional letter, a vowel . . . .

At first, no one noticed, but then a car turned around.
Later, a police cruiser slowed down, & then another.
A reporter stopped for that infamous photo that appeared in *Time*
& the first of a hundred interviews I declined,
& neighbors gathered. My phone kept ringing off the wall,
people yelling "bastard," & "traitor," & "get it the hell down,
or else." . . . Eventually, my best friend came to my door
& asked me why. I explained, "I can't explain." Others followed,
& insisted. "No comment," I said. "I don't want trouble,"
I said. "Read Hawthorne's 'The Minister's Black Veil.'"

I still like the way the black bow & ribbons flutter,
stark but suggestive of comic dark, serious, direct,
my own American allegiance & patriotic light.
Parson Hooper had his reasons, & half understood them,
but when he slept or spoke, his breath trembled the veil,
& even holy scripture seemed filtered by the terrible
transformation of black crepe into symbol. In the end,
not even his creator could commend the visionary parson
who espied the truth that separates & condemns.
Above my village, this beauty of black bow & ribbons.

39. (The Job)

1.

In March of 1968 when Charlie Company at last withdrew
from the village of My Lai where,
casually brutal, they'd tortured, raped, slaughtered, buried
innocent unarmed civilians by the dozens—

after they withdrew, Lieutenant William Calley & the rest,
they spent that night, & we with them in spirit,
in a Vietnamese graveyard, our sleeping bags & weapons strewn,
then & now, amidst stone lanterns & shrines.

2.

In March of 1991 after our elite technicians left off
incinerating defenseless fleeing defeated
Iraqi enemy & banked away from thousands of meat fires,
the charred & gaping human forms grilled out

along a 60-mile corridor north of Kuwait City, we at home gathered
to sing "God Bless America" & the questioning
"Star Spangled Banner" & prayed thanks that we'd gotten the job done,
whatever job it was, we try to remember, poppies & ribbons.

40. (Storm Coda)

1.
March 4, 1991: arrived at midnight, an ice storm,
worst weather here, or anywhere else I've ever lived,
of the century. Woke in the dark to thunder
of trees cracking around me. Brockport without power
today & for days to come. I'll be fortunate
if the great elm beside our garage holds firm
under the weight of the next 24–48 hours
of freezing rain & sleet. I walked out twice

to one open place at a crossroads & heard what
seemed like cannon shots across the treed lots,
& emergency chain saws from all directions.
The cold deepens, & the dangerous thickness of crystal
& diamond. In my yard, I scattered fifty pounds of seed
while mourning doves, a pair of cardinals, juncos, sparrows
darted in by hundreds among the fallen & falling limbs.
Where & how did any survive the night, I wondered . . . .

2.
Today or yesterday, under a tent somewhere
in the sand, occurs/occurred the ceremony
of surrender. Here, apple pie & a thermos
of blowtorch coffee with neighbors for company.
Later, kool-aid & cold spaghetti & the oblivious
imposition of hawk-talk going in one ear
& catching in my brain like an arm hung up
on a branch over a sparking wire. Just before

ceasefire, thousands more Iraqi dead,
the last killed when our dutiful technicians
cluster-bombed blocks of defenseless tanks,
bikes, carts & luxury cars fleeing north from

karmic revenge for their own tortured & murdered victims.
Here, ribbons coated with inch-thick ice,
or blasted or tangled in fallen trunks & limbs,
or stripped bare from trees in explosive cascades,

3.
or impaled, or buried. I've constructed this coda
by the light of a cedar-scented candle.
Over my village, a ribbon of siren wavers in nightwind.

41. (Epilogue)

1.
From its crowded clump in the wood, I transplanted
a six-foot cherry sapling beginning to bud.

I'd meant well for it, had pruned its branch-tips,
had dug it an ample ball, had lugged it in wet burlap

to my ice-freshened field, had tamped it
into a loam bed, had staked it, watered, it,

circled it in my hands several times for a long time,
had blessed it or at least prayed thoughts for it to blossom

from our warming Brockport winters for a century or more—
& then stood off a ways, smug with ideas of oxygen & nurture

here on this acre meant to balance the depletions of my own life.
But the tree never took. I waited weeks, a month, three,

sliced my thumbnail into twigs drying out despite
sequences of showers & all hosannahs of spring sunlight . . . .

2.

That was the year of our first war in the desert
from which we returned to amnesiac parades

in our marble capital & under tickertape blizzards
in the canyons of New York: while dozers still censored

hapless Iraqi fodder across those burning lands:
while a half-million children would yet perish

from baffled American intelligence & skill
& relentless play. O Father in your Xian heaven,

when did we not mean even to mean well, if not then? . . .
That was the year of our hundred-day slaughter

when spring, with no reason, in Your inexorable wisdom
just the same, despite the single harbinger

of my dead sapling, deployed itself again, transcendent,
to fuel my fossil heart, & you did nothing to stop it.

from

The Angel Voices

(1997–98 / 2010)

& in spring

furrows running
haze lifting
into sun
chicks scratching
in straw
in wet barnyards

trees again
done with our penance this
custody of the eyes the way
the rooted ones
last autumn
cast down leaves as though

in sympathy
or ashamed of us
to become
severer excellences
tell me
down on our knees

do we see them
Father Hopkins'
bright boroughs
of firefolk
heaven's breast
our Father

among the dead
are You there

Beauty

up north early
the red-notched
male redwings' wings
stigmatic
& pure silhouettes of black sheen swaying
on reeds the marshes
in their novitiate again
if this is beauty then
in our loneliness
how porous
the skin between
ourselves & our world-to-be
we do we
remember beauty

& furrows furrowed

forests into fields
to drain off
human fat
the pyres congealed
with firefolk
villages of them
cities of them
the chicks yellow globules oily
small wonder this
discipline of the eyes
the smell of it smell ye
the smell risen
do we hear
can we
are they ever there
have been
the angel voices

Irises

on an earlier altar
is this
beauty or
when I wheel-
barrowed thousands of eyes
up a slope their

colorlessness
spectrumming
memory tried not
to see them
see me
but the envased

cut flowers
scented me out now
insist that
which can-
not be spoken which
happened

Meadow ruptures

frozen upswell
rivulets
& barnyard chicks scratch
graineyes
in thawing mud
bits of yellow
you dead ones
distance yourselves curse
the sun just one cornkernel
moon wan
in the daytime sky cold
pustuled face
keep distance
springtime

Between our eyes

& the spruce
in the distance
snow sifts not
boneflakes but
snow but
does not stick

drains into rivulets into
darker shades this
regression our only
travail today
to keep distance
from the ravaged ones

Alabaster yet

breasts milksoft
between which
my vulgarity
angelic unction of
sounds trying
to become words listen
the sough & sign the
nipples held
inward my shaft
moist trying

to speak this muse
closes her lips
tremulous I
stare with my
reluctant
third eye into
Ursprung
the source she
her shudder
festers in me

But still a virgin

& a rib broken
began singing not
songs soldiers knew
two raped her again
all the while even hands
muffled her mouth
she sang & sang & would
not stop delirious or
mad or arrived now
among the angelic orders she
her painsong a soldier
raped her again released
himself in her then
shot her in her side she
sang he shot her her
breast wept blood she

raved song they
shouted their fear
the bravest coward
among them hacked
his sword bayonet machete
across her neck thus now
may he never
escape her
melody their punishment
doesn't it not
they return
the angel sings for them
may this come to be
tortures them with her
& for me if I were ever
could I ever be
could I be pure
song

Paul can you

your lyric locate
the thus non-transfiguring
source of starlight
the stars dead
absence arrives we
remember their story

stitched onto coats into
smocks onto uniforms
when we close our eyes
whence the light
can you begin your fingers
across catgut strings but

can you begin
again your strength
from such as this
uncreation's
retroaction thus un-
raveling becoming

never-was
never-to-be
only then
belief may sew
itself in you
in me

The dead

wandering off
into Time let them
speak consolations to one another
as only they
the blue flowers they remember
a blue dress
fruit trees first

awash in bloom then heavy
with biblical imaginings &
animals yes
yes & bread & the stew
who are we
to think we can ease them
understand let them
their hands around
someone's waist or over

yes shoulders let them
hie on their way
violinists blacksmiths
loafers teachers
across these fields
unto death the green
keeping of what they know
forest shadows
their ancestral songs
further away for the better
the closer but
for once for us
at least now is it again
despair our yes
from now on
compromised spring

A corpse its eye

crazed hellward
ditch in the brain
running with human fat
how high the words are stacked

layered wood & flesh
creosote pines pitched
stuttered hickory
burns fiercely & long

if only light were ashamed
of its forced revelations

if only wood were ashamed
of its forced offices

fat boiled off the bone Lord
if only You had sickened
& struck if only
Your ravens had clawed

the murderers' eyes leave
this place go to them
I want to be alone
without You

Even when

redwings flare
milkweed pods loose aerie
angelic whitenesses
over their fields even when
that which passes
passes away even
then history now
the burning children

perpetual revelation
fly through one another
beak & wings breast-
bones spring
speak nothing
that cannot be spoken
in their presence
but You do

Celan writing to Nelly Sachs

you're getting
better—I know, I know it . . .

please write again. It's going
well for us, Nelly, really well . . . . Yes,

it's bright again—the net, the dark one, is
pulled away—isn't that right, Nelly, you see it now,

you see you're free, in the clear, with us, among friends?
And I see even the words waiting for you, Nelly,

the words you give life to with your new
brightnesses—to all our joy

but Sachs could not believe him
who did not himself believe him

I so long for my beloved dead
I so long for my beloved dead

Ē

bowels viral
rotten *unterhosen*
spurts of shit
spatter down the legs
beauty the long ēēē the
lyric throat
Father Hopkins as he died
"I am so happy"
string-gobs of it
down on their knees heads
down over sloppails
soupbowl swill that which
heaves

Paul drowning

the monotone lung-
filling Seine
letting himself go
unto the not—
to-be-named
unword
exsoulment
the cleaving this
defusion this
repeated death
of his death-in-life this
exact instant
prefigured
ex-*und und* ex-*und*
ex
in You

Celan his late forties

brevities of joy
undercut
shrill laugh broken
a sick man
violucidal
the city of lights
charring in him
'they're experimenting on me'
the Seine still
a sluice in him

Masada aria
groomlight shimmer
dovegray breast-
feather water
at last & how
do we pray for him
do you
should we
to whom
pray for him

Orpheus

can you sing
your lyre locate
the non-transfiguring
source of starlight
arriving we
remember their story
stitched onto coats onto
smocks onto skin
numbers their
uniforms when we

close our eyes whence light
itself dead
can you your fingers
access these strings but
can you begin
again your strength
from such as this
stricken the particles
the children
the streaming

Dickinson's *shall*

translator Paul
her tongue in his mouth
enacted upon earth
we *shall* not wish
until death
to love the dead
beloved one
he hears her hears
her sister Nelly
I so long
for my beloved dead
why God are You
taking them
with us there
still here

Trumpets a shofar

shouts yellow
into the promised land
yellow pondlilies
my dreaming
drawing up
into yellow pads & bloom
globules of floating fat even
dragonflies buttery
veinsnakes entangled
pondmind afoul
with blanched fires
sun distant & yellow I
cannot hear
the few words seeping
upward into yellow air
can they surface
forgive me
sigh out

unvacuumed
stars in the day sky
yellow wax what does
not sicken dies I leave
that place swim through
gradually
greening reeds

Downstream now undertowed

Paul leaves us these
voices needles to stitch
illlumination over him
dazzling shroud

his last coat
could it have been
Father Hopkins' Jerusalem
this far too far

downstream

Hereafter

the abyss You
lost text
wingpetaling
cotyledon turning to the sun
the sovereign
rain glazing
tulipmouths
birdtongue pistils
against exile
a grandchild's arms
scenting my neck the
despiteness
deluded sunshine
turn under
that which does not pass

Thou mastering me
before us the
black covenant the
poets keep or else
the world as it is
all of it
were corpse

I would have us gather

we the departed ones small groups
outside in aftertime
tents cottages stone ruins
gusting fires
beneath trees
flicker our faces
to recognition
Sachs Crane Hopkins Celan

carefree we the translated
to hear & now is it
the angel voices or
You clear Your throat sing
their safety now
all of them their
palestine their
retroaction into

unbeing but
suffer their poems
here still still here I
would hear them
extant text their
never-having-been
and/or before Your
understanding Your
first & last prayers

A quieting this

snow settling
into early evening
so softly we wonder
if it exists except

for the past for
memory as it dreams itself I'll
start a fire touch
match to headlines under kindling

wrist-thick sticks ready then
mapleslabs I'm glad just
to stay home my wife
with me we'll watch

which movie nothing
too darkening then
Times Square a globe of lights
from that starvacuum

over the crowd whole
villages of them free-
falling into You
at exactly midnight

Afterword

In 1926 Hart Crane wrote to friends that as he was working on *The Bridge* his poem was "becoming divine" for him. His phrase of course assumes art's sacral nature, but also reveals Crane's desire to serve as instrument through which god/ spirit might speak. We can imagine this poet during composition, rapt, listening with receptive intensity for the sounds that might form the song of god's epic of the New World. He himself was bridge, spanning, strumming.

I first drafted *The Angel Voices* during the winter of 1997–98. I've cut out many sections since then, have added several that seemed to appear seamlessly while I was re-reading, and have revised in states of reverie year after year, feeling in control and in thrall at the same time. As close as I've been to it for a decade, I'm still not sure what my poem has become, but do know that while writing it and while reading it I've sometimes felt that it was "becoming divine." It sometimes seems to me now to be an audition, one hymn following another without forethought but with some kind of intuitional inevitability.

I don't remember where I read of the girl or woman who was raped & murdered so horrifically (and here keeps being struck with sword bayonet machete) but who, until her last breath, "raved song." It seems as though this is what, in sympathy, I wanted to do: rave song despite an event that could, or maybe should, stop our tongues, stop poetry itself. In "But still a virgin" the victim's song is beyond the rapists'/murderers' understanding, but does this song, in the end, become punishment for them? Song as her only recourse, though it cannot stop evil. Song as memory and conscience that will never allow the perpetrators to rest? Wishful thinking, maybe, but . . . the angel voices . . . .

I read somewhere that if we want to stay within a luminous dream, we should try to invoke a guide. Reading *The Angel Voices* now, I see that I turned to Father Hopkins to stay with me as I began to dwell on an atrocity image that instigated and haunts this poem, furrows dug to "drain off / human fat / the pyres congealed / with firefolk / villages of them / cities of them . . .". These furrows seem to become rivulets, ditches, sluices, rivers, lines of poetry, as I listen now, years after the poem first began to come into being.

W.H.
Autumn 2009

117

from

Shoah Train

(2003)

Prayer

It is the 1920s. In Paradise,
on its podium in a library,
an unabridged dictionary
turns its vellum leaves,
words like this one

(*mana*)
appear in visitors' minds,
& we are the glad dead
who study & write here
in white gold light under

the muses' alabaster eyes.
Lord of Shoah,
may we remain in Eden
where all that transpires later
forgets us, & always will again.

The Annunciation

Munich's *Odeonplatz*, August 2, 1914.
Stone lions stare out across the square.
In the crowd of thousands—
a photograph exists—
one young man appears in a state of ecstasy,
mouth agape, eyes wide
& slashed with light,
as though, in these moments, a divine destiny
were being revealed to him:

in *Mein Kampf* he'd write,
"Those hours appeared like redemption
from the troubling moods of my youth,
and I am not ashamed to say that,
overwhelmed by passionate enthusiasm,
I had fallen on my knees and thanked Heaven
out of my overflowing heart
for granting me the immense fortune
of being allowed to live in those times.". . .

We close our eyes: disembodied,
chorus of witness, we float down
into that photograph,
surround the one riven:
he falls to his knees: we know
what is next, & next:
we look up to heaven in supplication,
but know, now, we are helpless
in this roar of light.

Chimney, 1950

My father said don't ask from such things.
He didn't want to hear it what's the use,
goddamnit, be quiet, & then we were or else.
His brothers were dead & the Jews never mind
& the war was over & this was America where
anything could happen & we shouldn't forget it.
What thinks you you're so smart, & he laughed.
He'd raise his hand, & threaten, but not hit.
What he did during the war: carpentry foreman
at Bethlehem Steel in Brooklyn against the Axis,
the bottom line. Germans make good Americans,
he said, but lousy Germans. He smoked
three packs a day & hid behind his smoke.

Dedication, 1939

The line of WWI veterans,
my mother's father among them,
stood at attention on a Bremerhaven dock.
Gusts of brine wind lapped
at the Fuhrer's black leather coat,
but he took his time,

took each man's hands in his own,
thanked each for his sacrifice.
He of the luminous wounded blue eyes,
seeing my grandfather's
prisoner-of-war medal, asked where,
& how long. "Russia, two years,"

my grandfather answered,
then added, "I escaped."
His beloved Fuhrer embraced him
in moments of blue flame.
Behind them, *Das Reich*,
their new battleship, loomed.

Roof

In a photograph in the Auschwitz-Birkenau State Museum, prisoners
in striped uniforms, during the winter of 1942–43, work
on the roof of the underground
undressing room

of Crematorium II. We see six or seven, & a guard,
lumber forms, a cement mixer. The prisoner
closest is bending over, looking
into his shadow,

his right arm extended to a grid of steel rods over which cement
will soon be poured. He is thinking of . . . but
who knows what he is thinking?
& who knows

what terror will be lived below him? This roof-
in-progress above victims-
to-come where we
cannot

hear their prayers, their consolations for one another, as they tied
their shoes together, placed their clothes
on hooks whose numbers
they'd remember

to the end, if we could help them, if we could stop this . . .
but the cement mixer, on iron wheels, re-
volves its irreversible black urn
into the future.

Fugue for *Kristallnacht*

Around the corner where I lived a beautiful synagogue was burning.
Around the corner where I lived. Around the corner.
A beautiful synagogue. Was burning. Where I lived.
Around the corner where I lived a beautiful synagogue was burning....

My father came home in the evening I didn't recognize him.
He didn't want to talk and didn't talk what happened to him.
Was burning. He didn't want to talk and didn't talk.
What happened to him. A beautiful synagogue where I lived.
He didn't want to talk and didn't talk what happened to him....

Will they kill me is not so easy to forget either.
I didn't recognize him. Came home in the evening.
Around the corner where I lived will they kill me. Was burning.
He didn't want to talk. What happened to him.
Will they kill me is not so easy to forget either.
A beautiful synagogue was burning. What happened to him....

We packed the little things what we could carry.
My father said we didn't know where we are going who
will live will die. He didn't want to talk.
My father came home in the evening I didn't recognize him.
Will they kill me. Around the corner where I lived.
What we could carry. We packed. Who will live
will die. Around the corner a beautiful synagogue....

I didn't recognize him. My father. What happened to him.
Was burning. Will they kill me is not so easy.
The little things what we could carry. Was burning.
Around the corner where I lived a beautiful synagogue was burning....

(for Angie Suss-Paul)

126

Bloodhound

At Berchtesgaden a woman complained to the Fuhrer
she'd seen some Jewesses mistreated in Holland,
taken from their homes, forced into waiting trucks.
He shouted at her, "Do you not understand?
Every day ten thousand of my most valuable men die,
men irreplaceable. The best. The balance, then,
no longer balances. The parity of power in Europe
no longer exists if the *others* do not cease to be.
If they lived, those in the camps, those *inferiors*,
what would be our Germany in a hundred years?
I am accountable to my people. To no one else.
If I am branded a bloodhound, so be it. I care
nothing for posthumous fame." His relentless blue
eyes severed her. "You must learn to hate. *I* had to."

Pleurisy

My wife's Meissen brooch—
gift from her father when she was two,
1942, before his train to Stalingrad:

oval of porcelain hand-painted
with flowers of several colors,
framed in a lace of sterling silver.

Hansjörg Greiner was captured,
died of inflammation of the pleurae,
intricate membranes lacing each lung,

blue flowers blooming, taking all his air
who disgorged blood until dead . . . .
Hansjörg, those Jews you helped

get rid of, your Tübingen professors,
did you, after your death,
did you redeem yourself

within their forgiving curriculum,
or do you burn in Time,
hellflowers' flame?

The Gift

My mother-in-law remembered
waiting for her *Wehrmacht* husband
inside a station near Berlin.
A locomotive thundered in
hauling a dozen cattlecars.
She thought—she was not sure—
that through the waiting room's glass
she heard people moaning.
She tried to exit to the platform,
but guards kept civilians inside.
She did not smell anything unusual,
she told me, but did see hands
beseeching the air through slats . . . .

Inside the station, for several minutes,
an atmosphere of extreme tension
until the train departed . . . .
Later, her husband, future Stalingrader,
said that, yes, those were Jews
who preceded his own arrival,
one of many shipments to come.
He explained that, on this matter,
he forbade discussion.
She remembered that occasion
by his gift to her, a necklace
of expensive amber beads
with sea creatures caught in Time . . . .

Ghosts

Just once she allowed me
glances through a tin of papers
kept under shoes in her closet.
I saw an order signed by Himmler,
memos from the Ministry of Propaganda,
records of her Aryan ancestry
back to the eighteenth century . . . .

I don't know what all else I saw.
After her death, the evidence vanished,
probably burned by her widower,
American soldier who married her
four years after the death of her husband,
prisoner-of-war in Russia.
I picture him incinerating papers

one by one in a pot-bellied stove
in that rural kitchen.
Who is alive, & who is dead?
I married a German daughter.
A soldier opens the grate,
removes papers from this tin &,
one by one, thrusts them in.

'Christmas Celebration of *SS* Guards in Neuengamme'

On page 1058 of *The Encyclopedia of the Holocaust*,
at the center table, fourth down on the left side,
artless face resigned to the camera,
myself suddenly back to my previous life.

I now know that I knew: my camp is poised
for large transports, Jews from Hungary & Poland.
Mein Leben ist vorbei .... Of dozens, at this instant,
no one is smiling. Thus I hate our prisoners,

even the dead & dead-to-come, hate us all
& myself seeing myself here, a Heyen head ....
But this is Christmas: candles set in tall tapered
ceramic canisters incised with hearts;

bottles of wine in front of us; & what seem
angels in bursts of glare against the back wall O
I know how long I've lasted, wandering spirit,
& will. I would get drunk that evening, &,

in barracks, remove my boots as though they were
a mummy's leather skin, & sleep, & wake,
disgusted, sick of the wine, *und* cake, *und* camaraderie,
und schnapps, *und Arbeit*, . . . but then get on with it.

Euthanasia Economy

Dr. Hermann Pfannmüller,
Munich hospital director,
showed visitors infants
targeted for death,
those considered a burden

on the health of the nation.
In one instance a nurse,
as Pfannmüller lectured,
pulled a baby from its crib
& displayed it upside down

as though it were a piglet.
This would not be fed,
he said. It would take, at most,
two or three days
for the desired result.

Schnapps

Reports in Dresden, November 1944,
of mass murders of Jews in the East.
The troops had to be issued schnapps.
Some had committed suicide, some before
& some after their special actions.

It's time now, isn't it, for us to drink?
One schnapps for this memory,
& one for this; one for you, one for poetry,
one for me, & so on. Our nostrils detect anise,
our heads begin to drowse in sweetness . . . .

Tell me a story, a story of long before
when tresses swam in Germany's golden rivers
& heroes paused at the shore on their steeds
in legends before the slaughter of innocents.
We will forget. We will click glasses.

Milk Silhouette

On the prisoners' night march through winter,
one saw a milk can leaning against a tree—
she ran for it, hoping there was milk in it,
but a guard caught her, struck her

to her brittle knees in the snow, then, wearily,
unstrapped his rifle from his shoulder. "Mercy,
mercy," she pleaded. He fired through her fingers
into her face, then kicked her aside, empty.

Testimonies, 1946

Yes (Udell S.)

As one of my comrades worked,
an SS man approached him with a gun
and asked him if he had thirst.
Of course he replies, "Yes." So the SS

called over a second comrade, a certain
Tshernetsky from Bedzin,
and shot him, and then said,
"Here, now drink your brother's blood."

Coal (Kalmen E.)

The German said for two people
to fill a railroad car with coal
and for two people to lie on the floor
and be covered. When they were covered

he laughed at us and ordered us
not to dig them up, they should
swim up by themselves, and if they cannot,
they can just stay there.

Fifteen Germans (Isaac W.)

We also killed many Germans,
because they came after us.
We kept a pistol in our hand,
this way—he shouldn't notice.
And when he came close and said
we should hold our hands up,
we killed him. At that time,
we killed fifteen Germans before
they could search us or kill us.
We killed them right away,
and we went on.

Wounds (Jurgen B.)

People dead from phlegmonous suppurative wounds,
their beds overflowing pus,

would be lying next to somebody whose illness
was more benign,

who had just a small wound which now
became infected . . .

*[as here, in these constructs, these spaces
become infected.]*

Roundup of Children, Lodz Ghetto, 1942 (Israel U.)

I came to the tall wall of the cemetery.
Near the wall was a pile of coal.
I got between the tombstones.
There I was safe for the moment.

I heard screams of the children at night.
We hid out. In the morning,
they came and searched the cemetery.
The Germans went around with machine guns.

A few more days passed.
We were five persons.
We were in the cleansing house for corpses.
The Germans searched there, too.

We hid in an attic three days.
Later, the deportation stopped.
We returned to the orphanage.
Nobody was there.

Beauty: A Prelude (Fela N.)

I can remember Irma Grese. I knew her personally.
I didn't know that she was called Irma Grese.
After liberation, I saw her picture in the paper.
These things have been written about, how she dressed,

and what kind of face she had, so I know that it was she.
I remember her very well. She did such terrible things.
Her face, you know, was so beautiful.
Large blue eyes and beautiful golden hair.
Beautifully dressed in such a trim SS costume,
and a stick in her hand, and with a large dog.
She would come to us every day, and before she arrived,
we had to wait three, four hours for her.
From eight to eleven o'clock in the morning
we were called to the camp square without washing,
without food, without anything. We had to stand there
in the rain and snow and frost, that was all the same.
Stand lined up, four or five abreast, until *she* came.

The Language (Hadassah M.)

In Auschwitz my block was right across from the crematorium.
I had occasion to witness everything. It was entirely open . . . .
The transports arrived there, huge transports. In ten minutes,
by the clock, we already saw fire coming from the chimneys.

We knew if the transports were of fat or lean people:
if black smoke came from the chimney,
it was a lean transport; if fat, there was a huge fire going
that could be seen from distances of ten kilometers . . . .

Chaos (Abraham K.)

One of these brothers was separated
and the capo hit him real hard.
That was a Jewish capo.
That torments a person.
It makes one a revolutionary.
Here he is a Jew, and he beats me.
He is the same as I am,
but because he was in the camp longer
he has to behave that way.
And I couldn't open my mouth.
It does something to a person
more than to the one beaten.

And then a German policeman
who had brought us to *Markstadt*
stepped forward and told the capo,
"I brought these people up here,
and didn't have any trouble with them.
They have only been here a few minutes,
and already you have beaten them."
It was sad to see a German
put himself in our place
and have more understanding for us
than a so-called brother.

Instinct (David M.)

I found myself in the cellar.
The cellar was about chest-high under water.
About ninety or ninety-five people were lying or standing in this water.

Those who were lying there were already dead.
Those who were standing had arranged the bodies of the dead
in such a manner as to stand or sit on them. Otherwise,

the ones still living would have drowned.
I did the same. I found myself a place at the wall. I dragged
two bodies which were under the water and arranged them

against the wall and sat on them. I remained in the cellar,
counting from that morning, exactly two days and two nights.
During this time, my friend who stood next to me drowned.

I was almost unconscious throughout these days and nights.
I just breathed instinctively. I just lived instinctively.
I had nothing to eat or drink, but was alive. Then, all at once,

they were yelling, "Out! Out!" From upstairs,
people came down, and all at once I found myself
in a room out of the water, and I was lying on the floor.

Ellipses (Helena T.)

Prisoners in railroad cars did not know where
the trucks were going, and those in the trucks did not know where
the railroad cars were going.... And then it started....
And the other thousand were gassed....

Presence

In German, *Appel* = assembly, *Apfel* = apple.
Appel, at Bergen-Belsen, took place at 5:45 a.m.,
sharp, or else. *Apfel* was not a tree, not

a branch, not a single bloom in which a bee buzzed, not
a single seed. Still, at *Appel*, one survivor survived
one whole interminable winter by visiting an orchard

in her mind, trees exuding their warm scents for her,
limbs bending low with fruit for her. *Appel* =
assembly, *Apfel* = apple. But when we next

bite into an apple & taste its juice, we will remember,
will we, *Appel* at Belsen, a woman enduring winter,
her *hier*, the repeated rollcall, *hier*, but elsewhere.

Parity

It is, apparently, a fact,
that in Auschwitz in its season
occurred at least one soccer match
between *SS* who ran the camp,
& *SK*, the *Sonderkommando*,
the Special Squad, mainly Jews
whose daily survival depended
on beating order into arrivals,
on shorning, sorting clothes,
keeping the ovens operating,
pulling corpses from the gas,
removing gold teeth, slashing
orifices for coins & gems,
disposing of ashes.

In *The Drowned and the Saved*,
Primo Levi says that the *SS*
could not have played against other
than these 'crematorium ravens'
of their own creation. Forced
to help kill their own people,
embraced & corrupted
by the satanic Aryan engine—
with these existed parity,
a logical opposition &
the conjoining of spirit
for mutual health & benefit:
Come, said the SS, *today
we must play.*

Voice

Ich bin Bugdala, I am Bugdala,
boxing champion of the *SS*. Why
summon your superior to testify,
Heyen? If I could lay my hands on you
as on another Sachsenhausen Jew,
you'd regret you had the balls even
to write my name. Then you'd stand,
if still able, at the wire electrified
for sentimental filth like you, and,
if Jew-wise, thrust your cut cock
into it and fry. The beatings I administered,
the deaths delivered—all deserved,
all justified because such blood
defiles my Fuhrer's dream. Circular
are the corridors of Time through which He
still rages and inspires until the future
embodies us again. I regret nothing
except the too-slow footwork
of such a second coming to the world
as will redeem the German sacrifice.
Jew lover, I have your temple in my sights.

Almond

Herr Professor Doktor Heyen,
meine Name ist Maria Mandel,
SS, Auschwitz. I place myself here
in your imaginings by free will
to speak something from where
I have pulsed and circled in starlight
for what seems a thousand years,
or no time at all. *Mandel,*
yes, I'm almond—and as a child
I loved *Kuchen* with honeyed
slices of almond, as though, yes,
my surname were prophecy and fate.
Yes, I led children to the gas,
sometimes caressed the cutest
to calm them, but prodded
the frightened ones to speed them

to their Jewish state, their god
in the clouds, their palestine.
Did I lose sleep? For these
not worth whatever cost
the Reich incurred in bluish pellets
or injections of cyanide,
that bitter almond?
Herr Doktor, with your education,
surely I'm within your understanding:
the children would have grown
into more than harmless vermin.
We unsung heroines ask to be forgiven
only our incompletions . . . until we return
like almond trees in spring,
so beautiful and thirsty
to resume our destiny again.

Perpetrator

Who is this *SS* who carries out a newborn,
holds him or her upside down in the sink,
turns on the water & sings, "Here you go,
little Moses, down the stream," & drowns the child?

For once, we will not let this *SS* disappear.
We realize him there as he commits this crime,
bent to his task in his aura of evil, . . .
but as we do, the victim suffers, water

clogs its nostrils, it chokes & goes brain-dead;
nevertheless, we will not let this human demon
disappear. Will we? But this is almost, is it,
too much to ask. The *SS* says it again, croons

"Here you go, little Moses, down the stream,"
he is drowning the baby, we cannot bear to watch, to hear,
we are grateful his back blocks this scene.
He sings his lullaby. We must let the baby die.

Child

Kovno ghetto an *SS*
demands a mother's

he seizes
tears the child in half we

must/must not close
our eyes were

legs torn
wishbone was

body broken mid-
vertebrae is

to neck & the head
its eyelids was we does

memory is it
here we hear only

agony never
stopping the did he

fling the remains—
such volumes such

vacuum we
never cannot

the darkness under
the baby's lids

close this only do not
memory do not

the *SS* returns
memory do not

speak to us
do not not

nothing
to be learned here

we cannot bear it
or to be here

Auschwitz Reich Disfigured Haiku Sequence

Research
the 2-yr-old twin boys?
injection of chloroform into
their hearts

    the doctor's dissect-
    ing table polished marble
    w drainage channel

heterochromes: different-colored
irises: cut out
the twins' eyes,   float them in formaldehyde,
                      mail them to the Institute
                      in Berlin

    Flesh
    to cultivate bacteria
    in an electric
    incubator

        Phoenix
        after several days of stillness
        the ventilators'
        motors stir   furnaces flame again
                       as the Teresienstadt ghetto
                       offloads

teeth & jewelry
smelted—today 75 pounds
of pure gold

             burning bodies in a ditch
             50 yds long, 6 yds wide, 3
             yds deep

Heroism
a prisoner falls
onto a phosphorous bomb—selfish,
first to die

               ashes trucked to the Vistula
               fish eyes darkening

                     in the current

The Bear

Was alone, was carrying her bear with her.
Was alone, was carrying her bear with her.
Was alone, was carrying her bear with her,
bear to counsel, comfort, & protect her.

Arrived with a thousand other children
given toys to keep them quiet.
Was alone, was carrying her bear with her.
Was alone, was carrying her bear with her.

In the gas, her bear clawed free of her.
In the gas, her bear clawed free of her.
She held her bear as tightly as she could,
but in the gas her bear clawed free of her.

The mind & heart of her bear are wool.
The mind & heart of her bear are wool.
Its eyes black & shiny as tiny mirrors,
her bear is stuffed with wool.

Was alone, was carrying her bear with her,
its eyes black & shiny as tiny mirrors,
its heart wool, its mind wool.
Was alone, was carrying her bear with her.

Stones: The Efficacy of Poetry

Dissecting the old man, prisoner physician Dr. Miklos Nyiszli
found gallstones.

Knowing that his director, Dr. Mengele, was a most ardent collector,
he washed & dried them,

arranged them in a large-necked flask he labeled
with the subject's origin,

the kinds of stones they were, their characteristics . . . . The next day,
turning the flask

round & round in his hands, Mengele admired
the striated crystals,

then asked Nyiszli if he knew an old ballad about a family,
the Wallensteins,

who possessed many more gallstones than gemstones, *mehr
Gallenstein wie Edelstein.*

Smiling, Mengele recited several stanzas until that ballad,
his memories of childhood,

& the flask of colored stones lifted his mood, until
the assistant dared

request a favor: could Nyiszli search for his wife & daughter
who were here,

somewhere? Mengele agreed, & Miklos did find them,
& managed,

for a short time before the Germans murdered them,
to help them . . . .

Affliction

On August 17, 1940, Adam
Czerniakow, Chairman
of Warsaw's *Judenrat*,
visited the sanatorium
at Otwock.
He tells us in his diary
of being accosted
by a fellow Jew who
believed himself afflicted
with black candles
inside his body.

We see these, now,
from this far,
their flames
guttering inside him
black as the light
behind the killers' eyes.
How numerous these candles!
But they cannot,
no matter
how long they burn,
burn their way to surface

for Czerniakow the suicide
even after death.
The stricken—those eyes,
these candles that see
into us as though we were
instinct with them,
as though we could have helped
the candled ones,
&, the next time,
which will surely come,
will.

Ardor

Dr. Nyiszli sat with Mengele at a work table
perusing records on twins,

all that was known of them from birth to deportation,
to elimination, to dissection.

Mengele noticed a spot of grease on an otherwise
bright blue folder.

He leveled his eyes & voice at his assistant:
"How," he demanded,

"can you be so careless with files which I've compiled
with so much love?"

Mole

This many years later, a mole
tunnels into a mass grave,
only a few inches below surface,
but, yes, a grave.

The mole enters a ribcage,
progresses past a skull,
scrapes its claws
on desiccated bones.

The mole raises cursive mounds,
utters ignorant light,
searches for bulbs of wild onion.
Imagine its urgency of being, its

penmanship: *Nach Auschwitz,*
ein Gedicht zu schreiben
ist barbarisch. The soul
of poetry: raised tunnels.

Elegy

In his poem "Wooden Heart" Primo Levi stares
at a city tree, a horse-chestnut his own age,
but one, says this survivor, not ashamed
to bud & leaf in April, flower in May.

Roots crushed by streetcars, dog urine its rain,
deafened by noise, it grows twisted. The pores
of its palmate leaves clog with dust.
It would like to depart this place,

but year after year keeps sucking sustenance
from its toxic bed. Levi concludes:
Still, in its sluggish wooden heart
It feels, savors the seasons' return.

The survivor returned for more than forty springs,
then ended his own life, 11 April 1987,
but what of his companion? A tree
does not have a heart

(what we call heartwood is dead),
but did the tree, *does* it still in living memory
reach down into the covenant that every May
bursts with these red-streaked white blossoms?

Revelation: Theresienstadt Story

One June day, 1943,
Eva Roubickova, prisoner,
tended sheep on a slope
where there was a cherry tree with,
as she writes in her diary,
"marvelous red cherries."
She & the three others with her
kept watch as they ate these cherries,
which were not quite ripe.
Then she was standing there
with a branch in her hand
when *crack*! the whole branch
broke off. Of course,
at that moment an *SS* appeared.
Sabotage twice over, he said,
to eat cherries & to break the tree.
He picked up the branch,
handed it to her: "Here,
take the rest of the fruit.". . .

We expected a beating, torture,
her death on the spot
or at Auschwitz after transport,
but the *SS* said,
"If someone else had discovered you,
imagine what had become of you.
You're visible from far away.
For all I care, break off
as many branches as you like,
but don't let people see you."
The women started to cry,
relieved, touched that an *SS*
could still be kind.
"Even among Germans,
there are still humans," she writes.
That night, despite
diarrhea & stomach ache,
she thanked God
for that food on his hillside.

The Berries

Translucent red berries shine
from honeysuckle branches rising
above my windowsill. I'm reading
of a camp commandant playing
cards with Jewish women
before sending them to the gas van.
I picture him just whiling away the time,
until it's time.

This spring again, everything is in memoriam,
berries are drops of lungblood
floating in the breath of one
who was and/or wasn't there with them,
their God. One woman holds
a winning hand, we see her grimacing
up at him, at Him. Everything
hovers in place. I keep reading,

the commandant hears the distinctive rumbling
of the idling truck, & checks his watch.
He's enjoyed them, these women. *Schade,* it's a pity
he'll need to break in new ones,
most of whom won't know the game or be
competent, in their own turn,
to shuffle, to deal. He returns her smile.
He checks his watch again.

Star Song

By error in his dream the Jew Victor Klemperer
enters a café without his star.
Not even ersatz coffee anywhere, at least for him.
The star tortures his bosom

which is neither-nor there, nor here, unless
our language hears the source,
that sternum cosmos, that stellar dread in us,
our ersatz God in his fulsome nothingness.

Shoah Train

This train, for once, stops in an open field
before the railway station at Auschwitz.
Doors throw themselves open.
No one is here to guard the prisoners.

A scythe sweeps back & forth among clouds,
but, for once, its sound is not that of lamentation—
the prisoners look up but see only a curve of day-moon . . . .
They step out into meadow, even those already dead . . . .

This train gasps & wheezes as it cools, blows
a few last rings of smoke into ethereal air.
The prisoners spread their blankets & the food they've carried.
They laugh at so many flowers, & the stream that sings beside them.

There is no sign of anyone coming to get them,
either from the railway station, or deeper in the camp,
or from the future. For once, we are able, are we,
to leave the unfortunates there where they will never be taken.

The Presence of Absence

At a ceremony after the war,
at a ceremony to commemorate
French men & women who died in the Nazi camps,
French men & women & children who were murdered in the German camps,

sitting in the audience as names were read,
as names of many dead she'd known were being read,
a survivor, didn't she, heard her own name being read, heard
the several hollow syllables of her own name being read .... Stunned,

she raised her hand. She said, *Non, Monsieur, presente*,
she heard herself saying *Non, Monsieur, presente*,
she looked around & looked into the air,
she looked around

at other survivors & looked into the air's graves & smoke & heard herself
for once almost express the presence of such living absence
as she herself had become, *Non, Monsieur, presente*, ...
as she & they will always remain.

(Charlotte Delbo, 1913–1985)

Candy

All we could do was to remember it, to continue to deal in our memories, to create out of them poems and stories, history and reminiscences. It was the only way through which that irrevocably destroyed past could survive. Vilna had once been a red giant star in the firmament and had once illuminated the Jewish universe. It had now been extinguished. It had become a white dwarf star, emitting a feeble light visible only to those who knew of its existence.

Lucy S. Dawidowicz

I dreamed I worked in a shop in old Vilna,
there again this dim morning for the thousandth time.
First the boiling of sugar & milk in a large cauldron
over an open fire, then the stirring in of fruit syrups
with a wooden paddle. Was it you who helped me
carry the cauldron to a trough, & pour?

We kneaded the smoky mixture with our smoking hands,
then pushed it into a metal roller. Then the cutter.
That's all I remember, except for a huge map hanging
in the heavens, festooned with hundreds of tiny bulbs
where Jews had lived for centuries. The bulbs blinked
on & off for a while, then one by one blinked off . . . .

We taste them we taste them again, we taste them
we taste them again, we cannot not taste them but
for how long O we are among the last we
taste them we cannot not taste them their
living sweetness in this air with black tongues we
taste them in this dreamed dim light of old Vilna . . . .

You had left me. Where were you? Were you there?
I woke with the taste of red & green candies
in my mind, & in my chest a loss of light
sweet beyond redeeming—all that was left, for now,
of that city, until our next passage over cobblestones
through the feeble starlight of old Vilna.

ID

The Fuhrer's choppers—upper bridge set in yellow metal,
charred lower jaw with fifteen teeth—along with
his Iron Cross from WWI & dentures of Eva Braun:

last seen in 1945, in a cigar box, being offered
around a table of German dentists for ID.
This was the year of the liberation of Auschwitz

whose music was Mengele's, his conductor's baton
& singing scalpel. No way not for us to bite,
like teeth, clockwise or counter-clockwise, back to zero.

On an Injunction by Theodor Adorno

It is true that *SS* units at Auschwitz systematically gassed
     their fellow human beings.

It is true that during their long evenings they listened to Beethoven
     performed by Jewish prisoners.

It is true the musicians knew how the *SS* had spent their day.
     As the musicians played,

witches & ravens rose silently from their strings,
     & the conductor's baton

wrote this injunction in the air: *Nach Auschwitz, ein Gedicht zu schreiben
ist barbarisch.*

It is true these musicians are still playing. Never, always, never,
     will these musicians not be playing.

Bread

During the revolt in Crematorium I—
Auschwitz, 6 October 1944—
a member of the *Sonderkommando*
drew a knife from his boot

& plunged it into an *SS* guard's chest.
In seconds, two other co-conspirators
grabbed the guard, opened the door of my oven,
& threw him headfirst into the flames.

The Head

The interviewer asked the Jewish survivor,
one who had been tortured mercilessly,
"What does 'revenge' mean?"
Benjamin P. answered,

"For instance, I struck down a few people,
yes, killed dead. I, too, tortured
a few people. And I did the same things
with the German children as the *SS* did

"in Majdanek with the Jewish children.
For instance, they took small children
by the little legs and beat the head
against the wall until the head cracked."

He continued: "I got married in Judenburg.
We have a little baby, five days old.
A girl. And I have named her after my mother, Sara . . . .
A person gets adjusted." . . .

Visitors: Last Poem

when there are
no survivors left—
for only these /
may walk within
then, & this is now /
in this construction, /
let there be, north /
of the camp's main gate—
gate welded shut, for no one /
must pass through again—
an omission /
in the barbed wire /
as though accidental, /
as though storm-struck. /
let there be a raised /
granite path—
feet must not /
touch that soil—
a thousand meters long, /
diagonal, /
slashing the camp's grid /
toward the crematoria ruins. /
suspend this path /
over & along
the barracks' remains. /
no devotional stations
no inscriptions, /
no monuments. Let there be /
rectangles, /
open graves cut /
out of the walkway floor /
to frame fragments /
of what is left. /
let Time regain possession, /
grasses pull down /
even the chimneys: /
history must never /

be mere memory here. /
maintain only /
the guard towers /
& other perimeter structures, /
psychic geometry /
of perpetrators. /
being & not being /
of Auschwitz-Birkenau /
we will be selected /
to breathe it, /
to receive it /
as though it were /
what we were born for, /
forever. /
may the granite path /
remain for us our one /
abiding terror /
& question: what within /
our human spirit /
erupted here /
corrupted here /
exfoliated here

Barrow Sunrise

I grunt my barrow of eyes up a mud slope.
I'll empty them into a pit.
The eyes watch me.

At first colorless, now their irises begin to fill—
gray, blue, black, olive,
hazel . . . .

I tilt this volume of seeing forward. The eyes fall
into the pit, my barrow
empty at last.

Catbird

Another thick book of testimonies—
I knew I could not remember them all.
It was as though the survivors
were moving past me in a line,
& I were choosing among them:
that way to oblivion, this way
into a poem with my rhythmic baton.
But this spring morning a catbird sang
outside my door while I was reading,

while Rabbi Solomon H. remembered his son,
a nine-year-old who had,
Solomon tells us,
half the book of Psalms by heart.
When he was taken to be murdered,
he was saying the Psalms from memory.
Just before being gassed, the boy said,
"I am still going to pray to God.
Maybe at the last moment we will still be saved,"

& I looked up,
&, as catbirds will, this one
kept singing like crazy, its song
losing track of its beginning,
never the melodies of final meanings,
but going on as though nothing
within its own singing
could ever not remember
everything.

from

A Poetics of Hiroshima

(2008)

History

I'm reading history on a bench outside a pool.
An aluminum fence concentrates glare,
slants away. A child cries, *Erika, Erika*—
that's Erika on the diving board—then we hear

a shriek in air. But Erika's body is whole,
displaces water, surfaces. She swims forward
to where she can stand, extant in sunlight . . . .
It has taken decades for the murdered even

to begin to die, if ever. The *SS* are taking
control of the camps. History now
is like chlorine on innocent shoulders
to be showered away with chlorinated water.

It Came to Pass

that Josef Mengele realized,
as he stood at his station
conducting destiny with his baton,
that he himself was demon, son
of the scion of morning. He ordered
a cessation to the gassings . . . .

No, he did not. This was merely
a story that began to form in me,
in us, as though a new gospel
were possible, crematory skies
retroactive, bodies returned
to living beings. Tell me a story,

a poet implored, tell me a story.
I did. I had hope for the dead,
but Mengele, now, resumes
forming sounds with his baton,
one story after another, theirs,
but his, & his, & his.

Then: Ghost Story, 1944

Then it was spring at Birkenau. Cousins Dario & Morris
raised their hands, said they were barbers. Then
they were taken to a brick building, given shearing scissors,
led to a room packed tight with dead women. Then
their Kapo guard jumped up on the naked bodies,
boots & all. Then he demonstrated. Then

it was the cousins' turn. Then they moved too slowly.
Then the Kapo caned them. Then they sheared wildly until
one stepped on a stomach, this forced gas through the mouth,
she groaned, she near scared them to death . . . .
Then they learned their work, then came to witness
the mass gassings . . . . Decades later Morris testified,

"When they opened the door, I see these people . . . .
I see them all standing up. Some black and blue from the gas.
No place where to go. Dead. If I close my eyes,
the only thing I see is standing up, women with children
in their hands." Then for the rest of his life Morris heard
voices in his head calling out "God, God."

The Pearl Museum

Included in transports from the extermination camp at Treblinka in Poland to *SS* headquarters in Berlin between October 1942 & August 1943, last on a roster of plunder signed (no doubt proudly, patriotically) by Commander Franz Paul Stangl, were several thousand strings of pearls.

I know nothing of pearls in those days—just where they came from, how they were strung, how fashionable they were, how common or uncommon they were. Were some already cultured, grown from seed in tanks or roped-off seabeds? Were some already resin or plastic? Or were all still formed naturally in oysters' flesh as the bivalves coated grains of sand or bits of other intrusive foreign matter to render them harmless?

The Treblinka horde must have been of various quality & therefore of various worth to the Reich. They were a young girl's birthday gift; they were great-grandmother's heirloom string, lustrous for a hundred years, the silver-gray flawless beauties graduating in size toward the largest, pendant at center, & away. We don't know if the thousands of strings of pearls were classified by Stangl's jewelers, each placed in its own envelope or pouch, but, surely, they did not reach Berlin tangled like nacreous worms in a crate.

I would like to know what happened to the Jews' pearls when they reached the capital of the Reich, when they reached *SS* headquarters on *Prinz Albrecht Strasse*. Since only about 60 of 1,000,000 prisoners survived Treblinka, & since Stangl's list specified the far-from-precise "several thousand," did many strings that would not be missed go home that very evening to flatter the necks of beloved *SS* wives & daughters? In any case, most of the pearls must still be extant—one string in a safe deposit box in Rome or Lisbon or Zurich, another among a wealthy German woman's jewels in Hildesheim, a third at this very moment for sale in a shop in Montreal, another on display in a Manhattan window, a fifth . . .

It could be that particularly rare pearls were removed from strings for fascist redeployment in other rings, tiaras, necklaces. For the sake of their & our & the victims' souls, I would like the German people to make a census of these pearls, to trace each string & each separate pearl from time of seizure at Treblinka to its current whereabouts. I would like these pearls to be collected. I would like us to visit them in their own museum in Berlin or Jerusalem, these *Shoah* syllables, tier after tier of them in arks in dimly-lit sacristies where we could remember them even with our eyes closed, where we could listen to them all night long.

Museum Visitor Coda

A single can of *Zyklon B*
on a marble pedestal in a white room,
no other object herein, itself epitome
of 20th-century Germany,

its supreme artifact, industrial beauty
with which perfection achieves its name
in the burst lungs of Jews—the lovely
child Rachel, for instance, here standing

in line clutching her Steiff bear
that in the gas clawed free of her:
she held her bear as tightly as she could,
but in the gas her bear clawed free of her.

Sleepers

The child dies. The father
hires an old man to say prayers
over the body before burial.

The father falls asleep, dreams
his child tugs at his sleeve,
Father, I'm burning,

can't you see I'm burning?
He awakens to find
the old man asleep, & a candle

searing the arm of the corpse . . . .
This dream was told to Freud,
decades before the Holocaust . . . .

  Have we fallen asleep while praying?
  We enter the father. We suffer him
   suffering that cry,

   Father, I'm burning, can't you see
   I'm burning? He awakens
   to find us asleep & a candle

   sputtering in his child's arm.
   We try to extinguish it—
   no use. We cover the candle

    with sackcloth, but the candle burns.
    This, now, is our tableau,
    we sleepers who cannot waken . . . .

    The only movement now is candleflame
    under our closed lids.
    We are the wick, that corpse our wax.

Lullaby

A dream last night. A dream last night, I was standing behind a tall *SS* man who was drowning a newborn Jewish baby under a faucet. He was singing. I couldn't make out his words, not above the rushing water, but I knew what they were. He was singing, "Here you go, little Moses, down the stream." I knew these words because in my waking life I'd read them in a survivor's testimony in Henry Greenspan's *On Listening to Holocaust Survivors: Recounting and Life History.* The child had been born in another room just minutes before. Carrying it, the *SS* man entered where the survivor-witness was sweeping, held it upside down under a tap, turned on the water, & sang as though singing a lullaby as he drowned this baby—"Here you go, little Moses, down the stream."

I believe I was not that *SS* man in my dream. I saw his whole body from behind, was not fused with him—unless of course my memory of my dream censors it & makes it bearable for me; unless of course these perceived divisions between & among dream-personae are illusory. But, in any case, it did not occur to me in this dream to interfere, either, to try to save the baby. In my powerlessness as a reader of history, it may be, I had projected myself into the helpless witness that the survivor had been.

In Greenspan's book the witness did not say he had not seen that *SS* face, but I could not see it in my dream. The *SS* man's back was to me as he bent over the sink. I'm not sure I could see the child as he held it upside down under the water, but maybe, for just a moment, a durational traumatic moment that would abide in me, I did see the baby, right through that *SS* body, saw one of my own four grandchildren. At one time or another I sang to each of these children, "You are my sunshine, my only sunshine," a lullaby that always moves me. "I bowed my head and cried." But my grandchild would be with me there when I finished that song.

Apparently the survivor did not know the name of that *SS* murderer. Maybe he was a doctor, maybe an orderly of some kind or an officer passing through. He must have enjoyed what he was doing, & enjoyed his own obscene wit. Was he singing to himself, or to the sweeper? His song addresses the baby—"Here you go . . . ." The sadistic brainwashed brute holds the newborn by its feet under the water—this happened to happen not in Auschwitz but in Hamburg—& sings to it as he fills its nostrils & mouth & extinguishes it.

I have read a hundred Holocaust books, seen films, heard survivors speak in person & on tape, have immersed myself in that history, have had many nightmares over the decades as I've visited, only *visited,* atrocity. In all senses, I am shadowed for the rest of my days. I knew & felt this baby's death before, but this is now again the death that abides, no worst there is none. The beast of my own German blood holds the newborn upside down under the running water & sings, "Here you go, little Moses, down the stream."

Dr. Heim

In less than year after / being assigned to Mauthausen /
our Dr. Heim operated / on 540 prisoners, / amputated /
healthy limbs, / cut & left abdomens / unsutured /
to observe infection / & agonized death. /

One day he selected / two young men for their /
complete sets of teeth. / He himself injected them /
with poison, / then / decapitated / them /
ordered their heads / boiled & cleaned. / Dr. Heim /

displayed one skull / on his desk, / gifted / a like-minded /
colleague with the second . . . . // After the war /
we find him / in Mannheim / in gynecology . . . . //
Then he & his wife move to Baden-Baden to open

a practice . . . . / Evidence / of his war crimes /
surfaces . . . . // He escapes to Argentina for /
the remainder / of his works & days. // . . . What do I, /
for one, desire / to make of our Dr. Heim? / Need I /

know more, / or is outline / sufficient for me, / a German
doctor as exemplar, / the biblical / "mystery of inquiry"? / . . .
He enjoyed / fishing mountain streams, / attending to /
reveries / of his Reich even / while holding a trout before /

releasing it, admiring its rainbow / shimmer / from /
gills to tail / as though / it were / this very /
home here, / his name, / this poem / what I & he /
had always, / somehow, / wished / & worked for.

Poetry

I don't know the Lithuanian national anthem,
but know that at Kaunas in 1941 a murderer
climbed atop Jews' bodies with his accordion.
To hear him brought tears to patriots' eyes.

He is bloody from his work, but picture him,
& listen as the anthem swells. His wrists oscillate,
his instrument praises & swears allegiance,
many hum or sing along, his chords vibrate . . . .

Who am I kidding? You nor I can see or hear him,
nor can the dead though poetry would have it so,
if you know what I mean, which I sometimes do.
Kaunas recedes into the chords of that anthem.

All we hear *ad nauseum* is that history matters,
that we'll learn it or repeat it as the years
reveal our primal human face. Picture
the onlookers, their throats tight for their nation,

while one who clubbed innocents to death
squeezes air from those bellows, then
pulls his hands apart to draw air in again.
Take deep breaths with me, then try holding one.

The Word

I'll give you a hint: it rhymes with lice.
First, this:

Laurence Rees in his *Auschwitz: A New History* mentions
interviewing Wilfred von Oven,

once Josef Goebbels' personal attaché,
in 1990 a gray,

elegant, sophisticated man. Eventually, over tea,
Rees asked him if he

could sum up his experience of the Third Reich
in one word, what would it be?

"Well," Herr von Oven said, "if I had to summarize
my experience in one word: *paradise.*"

Anthem

As that murderer at Kaunas pulls his hands apart
to draw air into his accordion's bellows,
he seems to welcome us as though for an embrace.
Nor do his wrists pull straight sideways, but oscillate,

here, I'll show you, though this time I am not the one
who just a few minutes ago swung a club
that pounded innocent people to death. Like this, though,
my sinewy, muscular music swells, do you hear it?

For us, I grant us, that episode sounds very far away.
As I write, the sympathizers who heard their hero
play their anthem in triumph atop the victims
are themselves nearly dead, or dead, as dead

as poetry might allow the guilty ever to be, . . .
for here is our anthem now, played above them,
rupturing their graves to attempt to remind them
how their hearts filled with gratitude that day.

Exercise

& consider Ernst Krankemann, German criminal,
sent from Sachsenhausen to Auschwitz
to serve as Kapo,

1940. Krankemann, so fat he could hardly walk, squatted
on top of a giant roller used to shape
the square at camp's center.

Twenty or twenty-five workers were hardly able to pull it.
Krankemann, above them, whipped them—
"Faster, you dogs."

One evening, a prisoner collapsed & could not rise.
The fat Kapo ordered the others
to pull the roller

over the exhausted one, & they did, & heard what they heard.
We do & do not want to hear what they heard.
Krankemann laughed . . . .

Thus, I've orchestrated another story from the year I was born,
1940, even if even the most corpulent ones,
as this one of Krankemann,

cannot be birthed or thinned into knowledge, or even hate.
The obscenely obese sadist
rides my roller

over the square at Auschwitz as though born for it.
He enjoys it. It whets
his appetite.

History

Evening. I sat at the dining room table, working with tongs, sorting a shoebox of German stamps that had reached me a few months before from Switzerland after an internet auction.

I found dozens of glassines thickly packed with issues ranging from the 1850s to my own century's end. Below the glassines, too, were a few inches of loose stamps, used & mint. Thousands of *Briefmarken* in my horde. As I sorted, I was excited, alive. I realized that my American dollars had gone a long way.

As a boy I spent much time with my stamps. But now, sorting, a different childhood memory kept crowding in until I wondered why: hour after hour, I was at my microscope, tilting its mirror to catch the indoor or outdoor light, eyedroppering pondwater onto slides, staring, surprised by the dimensions I could keep focusing into view. Just when I thought I'd located every organism in a particular drop, another amoeba or paramecium appeared, or a grotesque & fearsome hydra that startled me . . . .

Now, time passed quickly. I was tonging various stamps into various groups. I mounted some in my albums, placed others in stockbooks, others in new glassines that I arranged in numerical Michel catalogue order in my files. There were the shield varieties of the early confederation, & many Germanias of the early empire, & a great many of the inflation issues of the 1920s, but I am most interested in the issues of the Third Reich.

I found several of the death's mask Reinhardt Heydrich, the "Blond Beast" whose assassination led to the annihilation of a village in Czechoslovakia, Lidice, & most of its inhabitants. But of all the propaganda stamps from this period, the greatest quantity were those of the variously-sized & -colored Hitler heads.

As I grew tired & my eyes began to cross, I hoped at least to organize all the stamps in this particular series, but it seemed that no matter how long I sorted through the glassines & then the loose stamps at the bottom of the shoebox—all this history emanating from the center of Europe—there was always another right-facing profile of the Fuhrer. Each time he appeared, he seemed smug, enriddled, immortal, not at all surprised to have reached light again, to have made his way even to America. Each time he appeared, I realized I'd never be able to isolate & bring into focus all the animals in this pond.

Illumination Graft

"a section of the hospital was used
for research into
the effects of castration followed

by cross-gender grafting
of the reproductive glands." . . .
"In the operating theatre,

illumination was provided by
several moveable lamps
and a large, fixed, central light."

If

If the Nazis had been left to their devices, if they had kept on,
as Laurence Rees phrases it, with "the process
of turning mass murder into an ordered profession"—
for think of Commandant Stangl arriving at Treblinka in 1942,
realizing that his predecessor's primary problem in making
the camp run smoothly was the capacity of the gas chambers
(bodies were littered all over, trains waited to be unloaded,
the stench was unbearable, the corruption & licentiousness
& frequent ineptitude among Kapos & even SS intolerable),
& think of Stangl building a much larger gassing facility with
"a central corridor off which ran eight separate small gas chambers,"
each of which "could be accessed from outside, which meant that
"clearing them of corpses would be much easier than before,"
total capacity becoming over 3,000 Jews, more than
six times greater than previously possible—
if the SS had gone on to evolve, had had the time
to perfect its process, again, to quote Rees, "of turning
mass murder into an *ordered* profession" (italics mine),
German universities might have offered a major in this,
German students might have received degrees in this,
with doctoral dissertations on various human fertilizers, on
efficacious recovery of jewels from particular orifices,
on pacifying vermin children during their procession into the gas,
on creating a hygienic work environment . . . as trains
kept arriving from further & further. Pre-Stangl chaos
was not to be endured. Professionals were needed,
an ordered workplace of which the Reich might be proud.

Sunlight

Within what Anthony Hecht calls "that domain of art" some have said say nothing Rabbi Irving Greenberg says say nothing that cannot / should not be said / that is not "credible in the presence of the burning children" / do they even exist or hear us these injunctions quail us / he does not say credible to *them* but we will let's not bore them not expect too little of them not fear to take chances coo or rave go wild with / for them tell them even their own searing stories—the poet Zelda asks "Are stories my fortress?"—even trust them to forgive us do they even exist Emerson wanted above all wildness from the poet after 'the child is dead' he said to little Louisa May Alcott who came to his door to inquire after his Waldo her little friend died five years old his father's grief yes of rued human "evanescence and lubricity" but his child was dead he could not it might be break out of his iambic wail / but these children were burning from lorries dumped at the Auschwitz pit the boy Eliezer Wiesel could not believe his eyes at pitch night his first day there in the German camp in Poland the Germans their language were burning children they'd murdered & even children still alive

    & locate Holocaust scholar young Raul Hilberg each morning for three years setting up a bridge table in his parents' NYC apartment writing in pencil chapter after chapter *when* would he be finished his mother asked him his father *when* would sigh now *The Destruction of the European Jews* revised & expanded the three slipcased frightcar volumes & now several decades later Hilberg's statement *The Politics of Memory* his "The words that are thus written take the place of the past; these words, rather than the events themselves, will be remembered" yes we've not wanted to know this matrix where art/poetry their maws open Hilberg within his work discovering "a primordial act that had not been imagined before it burst forth" Hilberg within his work listening to Mozart & Beethoven as he wrote creating *The Destruction* a work of art he said Claude Lanzmann told him that to "portray" the Holocaust we have to make art I hear so-called survivor Paul Steinberg in *Speak You Also* say "Those of us who couldn't bow low enough have long ago gone up in smoke" the poet will finally bow low enough to art as master won't he or die by the vertiginous compromise Walt Whitman says "Dazzling and tremendous how quick the sun-rise would kill me, / If I could not now and always send sun-rise out of me" so picture Hilberg up early and/or writing late at his parents' bridge table a graduate student hearing Schubert's Quartet in C "a Germanic work" he says & hearing Beethoven's *Appassionata* "that supreme achievement of piano music" as he raged / prayed for / intensified toward "overall symmetry" balanced harmonies e.g. he says "It was the *andante* of my composition, with a theme of multiple variations that mirrored the special conditions under which deportations were carried out in each country" we hear a fallacy of means here of form this "mirrored" just theory / voltage in writing is not electrified barbed wire nor my statics here but Hilberg composing/conducting his art-text no less than no more than a child at Terezin coloring a butterfly the Jews the facts of the Jews the suffocating vomitous shit-running data of deathtrains the Jews but the point is Hilberg's . . . radical . . . acceptance . . . that art was his meaning his theme did he always know this / when have *you* learned it / as the Germans conducted the Jews these children to the gas within Hilberg's uncovered schedules the *SS* officers that depravity Mengele with his chic faddish conductor's baton his symphony the lovely child Rachel held her stuffed companion as tightly as she could but in the gas her bear clawed free of her / she held her bear as tightly as she could / but in the gas her bear clawed free of her despite

Nach Auschwitz ein Gedicht zu schreiben ist barbarisch Adorno is of course correct the manipulations / resolutions / pettinesses / pretenses / artificialities / failures / loves or so-called successes of art remain obscene given the perpetrators acting out the horror of their natures their educations burning the children some alive burning pyres of families the *Mussulmen* digging ditches out from the strata necessitated sluices to draw off the human fat make some kind of music of these brain lobes these furrows? some kind of paintings? sculptures? poems? Adorno is correct who later tempered his tongue begrudged we needed to have our say I say Adorno was right to begin with & wrong & correct when he tempered his speech & wrong for here's Czeslaw Milosz that exile who said time came when he knew earth could not be his home nor any hereafter but here he is in *The Witness of Poetry* & he is correct & he is wrong he says "Whoever invokes genocide, starvation, or the physical suffering of our fellow men in order to attack poems or paintings practices demagoguery" / & then our next inevitable step toward our only hope our despair toward the supremacy of art as when Lawrence Langer recognizes the "void of discord" atrocity knowledge visits on us(my word, *visit*s, & the right one, I only *visit* these materials which yes always shadow me but I am visitor my grandchildren will visit me this weekend e.g. & we'll have light & air I only *visited* Bergen-Belsen the one *Konzentrazionslager* on whose ground I have in my body stood Anne I had your diary in me there, but we only *visit* in fact Erich Neumann in his essay "Meaning and Man" says "one million Jewish children could be slaughtered with no great impact on mankind—not on psychologists, theologians, believers or unbelievers, from the Pope to the Communists" he doesn't mention the poets but we too *visit* but some poems can stay longer can stay always that duration of art)—Langer knows we can no longer aspire to "the utopian humanistic enlightenment we once dreamed of achieving" but, but, but still says "no oral testimonies so far equal the *art* of writers like Primo Levi, Aharon Appelfeld, Charlotte Delbo, and Ida Fink to name only a few" he too on the visceral slope toward art whatever art no matter what despite its myriad pre-emptions / egotisms its sometimes semi-trances of illusory coherence despite its . . . *beauty* . . . / Fink's baker Weizkranz old & sick stuffed into a barrel the details endlessly varying as his story is told how he was rolled until dead he rolled unto death variations on a nocturnal theme this art while his camp's commandant after the war sells smoked meat & the kapo that "dog in charge of all the other dogs" becomes white-collar while Weizkranz is a kind of music isn't he our way toward the *the* of this melody's domain of barrel staves on gravel Fink says he "for maybe even years, will keep rising from the dead and dying in the barrel" notice "maybe" as operative word *maybe* if we can see/hear him can we will I or you or will we weary of/recoil from this flour-shrouded memory—in one of Fink's story-plays (a Jewish couple long in hiding) a woman says "There was an oriole who used to sing in our garden" but the man answers "Klara, no memories. Remember our bargain"—but how the baker enfigures himself into art-memory his strength from being shaped by the barrel the "paradoxical imperatives" in Jay Ladin's terms of its staves that musical form nothing no sound getting in to him except the sound of the crushing gravel the snails crushed underfoot at Glasnevin where Gerard Manley Hopkins is buried father the baker brings you his bread the kingfisher blood from his ear the music of this foot-crushed stave-crushed gravel don't touch me you brutal foot you bastard the form-enfolded Weizkranz the baker demands of me from his elsewhere tell me my story he regurgitates the nothing within him our art this barrel becomes him & churches are shells discarded by God in Ladin's poem "Snails" as our maker "with thorns and a single foot / . . . crawls over the world" / Weizkranz is it true your knuckles broke / your kneecaps / broke your clavicles / broke like snail shells underfoot & how the perpetrators hide in my own habitual syntax *they* your knuckles broke kneecaps clavicles the merciless ones the barrel of history crushed music into that gravel

    & how in *The Primal Mind* Jamake Highwater describes his efforts to discover "communicative accesses" toward breaking barriers between the dominant culture & the Other (what else were Lakota to the dominant culture but vermin?) could only be by way of "the metaphoric form of expression called 'art' in the West" he says "if someone does not experience an aesthetic relationship to what is before him or her, all the information and education will not permit that person to cross the distance that exists between different peoples" but what "aesthetic relationship" with smallpox blankets & bayoneted genitals but Highwater's faith & what else is it that we might aspire to except to / break down, break down again my songs where the lorry of murdered children draws up at the firepit the boy Elie needs us 50–60 years later in *A Jew Today* he'll write "If you have not grasped it until now, it is time you did: Auschwitz signifies death—total, absolute death—of man and of mankind, of reason and of the heart, of language and of the senses. Auschwitz is the death of time, the end of creation; its mystery is doomed to stay whole, inviolate" but despite art he keeps writing he resists writing he mentions Rabbi Mendel of Kotzk who was silent

even when speaking what is all this but a selfish defense of poetry which cannot /
can it be spoken *credibly* in the presence of the burning children do they even exist
my failure & you with me too in this "mystery" Wiesel says & Herman Melville's
biblical *II Thessalonians*, 7 phrase "mystery of iniquity" rises to him from beneath
John Claggart's black breastbone Jay Ladin's utterly forlorn & surrounding phrase "an
evil that beggars cognition" & *is* evil ineradicable our natural essence each cell stained
the smoker's lungs that will never regain the rose color of fleshly innocence even after
the smoker stops smoking for sixty years the crematoria or can Highwater's "aesthetic
relationship" as Hilberg composes *Destruction* be of some even slight assuagement of
the darker angels of our nature Satan of the darkest order I don't /can't know but do
know & the answer is *no* but know that the most encouraged I am in this history is
when I read that many brainwashed *Einsatzgruppen* went mad / committed suicide
could not after all continue / something of what we hopefully even prayerfully call
the *human* welling up in them after the first murder & after the 100th & 500th it
is not that there is no other but that the Other *is* another an other & the German
soldier sometimes despite Hitler *und Vaterland und* his drunken comrades broke
down from the radiant stain of his conscience may our natures now modulate ever
into benign forms is there time on earth will our brains allow us break down again
my crazed songs & for now give me joy you murderers of my own blood kill yourselves
you're human after all my only lifeline your suicides splatter your acidic hearts here
on my pages even while ours is Susan Gubar's poetry after Auschwitz please do I hope
in the end to locate myself there "this task of abjuring the redemptive paradigm" /
I hope as I abjure hope because of my hope nevertheless & may you be strong songs,
my songs worthy company in this mystery this "opacity" as Susan Sontag says &
may you be at least sometimes unselfconscious but true to me & may you be at least
sometimes poetry the black liquid that seeps from the muse's eye-sockets if I'd been
born not in Brooklyn in 1940 but Berlin in 1920 I'd have aspired to the *SS* from that
culture my German-born parents wished the Jews the worst I was a blonde youth tall
an athlete I'd have sworn allegiance to / murdered for / cut off my fingers for that
incarnation of Reich savior he of the "luminous blue eyes" as Goebbels wrote in his
diary on first meeting him how could / can I resist that blood-anthem hypnagogic
rapture for whom I'd raze villages slaughter innocents but then I hope get drunk
then I hope press the curved trigger-stave the barrel of my rifle against my shell my
raised temple & fire before he takes me here eat this new grotesque beautiful revolting
formful poem this visitor this /

Shoah Goat

My dream, the goat rears up on its back legs.
Come here in human moonlight, I cannot

see it straight on. Look to the side of it,
& to the side of the side of it, I can almost see it

but only so far as my fear allows—its leather
horns smoldering, its chin slavered with viscera,
its lurid cock shining with Jew-spittle & blood,
its cleft eyes blue & crossing now to remember.

I did not nor you we are not guilty must insist despite translucent possibilities
of fallibility & brainwashed complicity I did not was not there nor you we did not
murder the lorries of children dumped into the burning pit do not never we must
Anthony Hecht must not have thought this through misread who praised *The
Swastika Poems* for reaching "that domain of art in which criminal and victim,
caught in the light of a steady vision, are virtually the same" I'd beg the dead's
forgiveness but I did not write this no there is no such "domain of art" did I write
this / this is not May Sarton's journal entry "I cannot separate Germans from Nazis"
her sense however right or wrong or however to be modulated Goldhagen's argument
of national complicity but this says starkly Cain *is* Abel no I did not lyric this but
yes I have sometimes accused undercut recoiled from their God on whose assumed
keep they suffered who was not there with them or witnessed & did not lift an eyelid
to keep them Rachel held her bear as tightly as she could / but in the gas her bear
clawed free of her / break down break down again my songs / Whitman says despite
everything the half-holy cosmic one unexiled despite holding the young dead & dying
in his arms the piles of amputated limbs at Fredericksburg not withstanding his
imagination & soul sickness & being there says "I believe the soggy clods shall become
lovers and lamps" his own domain but goodbye Walt after the Shoah's deathcamps
we depart for our residence now the beloved child has not in his duration died of
Scarlatina but is murdered we reside exiled in Ladin's "revulsion against the very
texture of the aesthetic" for decades I didn't think so but in the end it's about me isn't
it? but let's stop stuffing this bear stop gassing it for who does not want even Celan
wanted with his imploded incandescence his backwhorling from *dass was geschah*
that which happened wanted & Levi who says in an interview he'd revise Adorno to
"after Auschwitz it is barbaric to write poetry except about Auschwitz" / & Wiesel &
Hilberg & Ozick in *The Shawl* & Jean-Francois Steiner in *Treblinka* & Samuel Bak
in his candle-crematoria paintings & Susan Fromberg Schaeffer in her novel *Anya*
& Joyce Carol Oates in her novel *The Gravedigger's Daughter* & Marcus Zusak in
his novel *The Book Thief* all wanted / want don't they or I'm deluded don't they at
once *both* in Gubar's terms want "heartfelt and personal reactions to the disaster" &
texts the same texts that cannot be fully sounded cannot be exhausted *will* in Ladin's

terms "invite & repay critical attention to the work they do" even as we know our best work our art only *visits* for now while weak poems puddle & imply they know / but art is now cadaverous with man's ultimate architectures the deathcamps after the Shoah we humbly/egotistically reside with this it could be when we become most human an unstylized knowledge this extremity of exile from the fields & trees of the oriole my despairing

Sunlight

This is what we've learned: victim
Miklòs Radnòti's poems
(the ones exhumed from a mass grave
after the war before their notebook could rot)

would have kept deepening if
left in the pit whose contents mis-
understood them but kept teaching them
that language we living can't speak.

Autumn Rain, 1946

Then Goering crunched down hard on a filling
under which a cyanide capsule burst.
Maybe a minute of agony, & then death,
at Nuremberg, on his own terms.
Those who would hang came to envy him.

Hermann had grown so fat that wolverines followed
in his shadow to gorge on him in case
he fell. No, they didn't. But he did grow obese,
& his huge hunting lodge filled with Third Reich swag.
O those unforgettable social evenings of elegance and grog.

You've heard the saying that it's hard to predict history.
I'm writing it now, as you are while hearing this.
Who knows who is going to say what about us
as time comes to pass? Of course, we'd both rather be
on the side of the seers, so please plan on revising me.

By now everyone knows that cyanide
permeates the corpse that smells of almond.
I heard that Goering died in his pajamas, with his boots on
that so often strutted beside the Fuhrer's
as rapt throngs witnessed their strides toward suicide.

Those were of course the finest Italian leather boots
Germany could afford. Their raised heels
shaped calves, thighs, buttocks into firm
Aryan shapes that a shapeless nation
might model. But our hero became so flaccid

that when he tried to dance at *Karinhalle*,
his prodigious hips & ass knocked over
a Picasso blue, then Rodin's *Thinker* who,
chin on fist, still ponders Hermann's avoirdupois
in contrast to the death camps' walking sticks.

History eventually placed that morphine addict in a casket
with his last-worn garments, & those boots. The casket
was sealed & loaded into a 2½ ton truck,
& driven away, under military escort that dissuaded,
with pointed machine guns, reporters or fans from following.

At Erlangen to the south, that casket was opened,
identity confirmed by American, French, British
& Russian officers. Cremation took place posthaste.
A black sedan sped in, picked up those ashes
which had been swept into a nondescript container,

& whooshed away—we're not sure in which direction—
into the countryside over pitted dirt roads & cobblestones.
All evening, a convenient historical rain had been raining.
An hour later, the Reich Marshall's odorless cremains
eddied into the drain of an anonymous village lane.

Iwo Dahlia

My high school coach of the mid-Fifties—
he brought us a dahlia, a single purple bloom
my wife and I have floating in a glass bowl on our kitchen table.
Add a couple ice cubes a couple times a day, he said,
and it should keep, as it has, except for corolla petals
now curling blackly downward.

A few years back he gave us a babyfood jar of sand from Iwo Jima.
With six hundred other veterans, he'd returned a half-century after
hitting the beach there, burying his face in this volcanic grit.
At Marine reunions, he can't find anyone from his old outfit.
Dahlia, that widower grandfather now trusts his memories to you.
May you distill color from even blackpurples, and remember.

Autumn means digging up their tubers, wrapping them in burlap,
carrying them to his rural cellar where the mysterious
dormant life in them will overwinter. They need cold,
but he'll check them several times to make sure the ice
or insects or mice haven't found them out.
There's no sump pump, and usually his hard-packed dirt floor—

I've been down there—retains an inch or two of rain,
but he's constructed a path of raised flagstones,
can make his way, he tells me, even without a flashlight,
through the dark to the cabinet where his dahlias sleep.
The promise of them again is always in his mind,
and has been, and will be, one way or another . . . .

D-Night at Iwo Jima was cold, the wounded shuddering,
medics brushing black sand from stumps and bandages.
Six hundred Marines were dead already—the Japanese
had sited their artillery onto the beaches months before,
were hidden behind revetments in mountain caves
and deep tunnels, were seldom seen that day.

Safe civilian litter-bearer, I'll haul Coach's dahlia
to our compost back of the garden, and spade it in, but not yet.
It will lose its colors, its seared purples going to sepia and black
as it edges in on itself, collapses, and begins to smell,
but not yet. For now, whole, it concentrates October light,
seems to sense the silver maple leaffall outside our window . . . .

Inland that first day, a medic plunged into a shellhole,
then looked around. Next to him, the detached arm
of a dead Marine, its wristwatch keeping time, gold band
shining in Iwo sun, 4,000 miles from Pearl Harbor. Dahlia,
transform to gold, keep memorial time. I'm standing again
above the *Arizona*: 1,000 dead, average age nineteen . . . .

Rear Admiral Toshinosuke Ichimaru, commander
of this island named for its springs of sulfur,
to venerate His Majesty the Emperor wrote poetry.
He prayed Hirohito live as long as sacred Mount Fuji.
Grateful to be placed where he could die
against the American assault, he wrote:

> *In the twilight the waters of Lake Hamana cool,*
> *Sending breezes to fill my garden,*
> *Fragrant with sweet oleanders in full bloom.*
> *Let me fall like the flower petals scatter.*
> *May enemy bombs aim at me, and enemy shells*
> *Mark me as their target . . . .*

Tonight, those petals scattered, rain seeps
into my teacher's cellar,
but he is there again, walking on flagstones.
He unwraps burlap and fingers the dirt-crusted tubers.
May he be able, long as he lives, to bear these dahlias
whose names are myriad, whose target is his heart,

but who can?—there is too much in him, all night
white and amber and green-suffused flares
color Suribachi, lives leak through gauze into black sand,
flamethrowers wait on the color-coded beaches in dreamfumes
of burning Japanese meat and the suffocation to be visited
on these unbelievers with revengeful biblical fury . . . .

In the jungle battles at Bougainville and Guam,
men died out of sight, sank into foliage and swamp quietly.
On Iwo Jima, men died in full view, torn apart,
their bones and viscera spraying and splattering,
shrapnel slashing into them as their last thoughts
flew toward the silence of the past, and home.

On Wednesday, the last day of February, 1945,
their tenth day ashore, the Marines held less than half the island.
Hand-to-hand combat in the central hills—
no survivor will describe this terror.
Where is the old man when he is in his cellar
and shuts his eyes and touches the cemetery of dahlia?

In spring, when all chance of frost is past,
Coach plants them in staggered rows, six inches deep,
one tuber per cedar stake, stakes two feet apart,
rows six feet apart so he'll have room to groom and tend.
You lay each tuber down, he says,
with its eye-end toward the stake, pointing up . . . .

The single dahlia head in its bowl sometimes
seems to weigh more than its table can support,
evening light fused with sepals and petaltips,
notes of taps lost in its empurpled and disfigured inwardness,
Time's harvest now, waking and sleep equal,
as though its presence were a cave being sealed from us.

The night sky lit with dead stars, a jugular vein pierced,
but a medic kneels to the panic, slits the bullet hole,
lays the vein bare and clamps it, stuffs the hole with gauze,
holds it tight. Lips pressed closed, he prays
that this day's battle be god's will. Enfold this tableau,
dahlia, succor the striken soldier and his savior . . . .

Wrapped in tissue in a small oblong box under shirts
in a drawer in a chest in a bedroom in a house
off a road in a town in a county in a state
of our country, under a ribbon and stars, George Washington
faces left in profile on a Purple Heart. He's thinking
of his wife and Mount Vernon. He seldom sees the light . . . .

I dreamed countless *sennimbari*,
cotton bands of a thousand stitches
worn around their waists by Japanese soldiers,
each stitch a prayer for their return.
I coughed a belt, a clot of *sennimbari*,
woke from a vomit of blood and magma . . . .

Can the dead remember, Iwo dahlia?
Where were you, what garden preserved you
when their ravines received the flaming oil?
From even this distance, from the safety of our grief,
you still smolder, your tuberous nature wrapped in burlap,
your eyes inured to that incendiary sun,

and sweet water, and the essence of the living who were there.
You depose the sacramental rose, do you, and the dooryard lilac
smug with pastoral remembrance, and the Japanese oleander
whose commander rhapsodized his suicidal honor.
Dahlia, you've lost your heavy heads to mortars,
your petals shrapnel the neck of our hourglass . . . .

Near the end, the fight in the northeast, a Marine lay over
a sulfur fissure, the hot mephitic stench
seeming to help stanch his fatal wound;
here, dahlia, bleed in your bowl,
enemies slash the ears from your helmeted head,
pull your teeth with pliers for souvenirs . . . .

Two months after D-Day a journalist visited Iwo, noticed
big blue flies clinging to broken limbs, "so numerous
and so close they almost touch. They don't hover or buzz.
They just cling. Brushing a limb barely starts them.
They just cling, surfeited." E.B. Hadfield deployed that word,
surfeited, as though the flies were fat and drowsy with gore,

the blue flies and dead limbs a grotesque parody, he said,
Iwo Japanese flower arrangement. Here, then,
the ceremony of dahlia: viscous lacquer pacific pour
of surfeited flies into a cup of porcelain hemlock
as Coach, asleep, or kneeling in his floating cellar,
breathes deep, and resists, but remembers . . . .

When the U.S. returned the island to Japan—1968—
Coach's dahlias surrendered in ironic gloom,
downcellar, in burlap, in his cabinet,
but fought above ground in full gear, but didn't.
He was with them when he was not with them,
living what had once been theirs, life in light.

Back on Iwo, lagged and blitzed, he rode a shuttle
up from crosses to the summit of Suribachi's cone
where bushes and grass camouflaged pillbox rubble.
He'd carried with him a dozen miniature Old Glories
and now pushed them into the mountain, stood at attention,
then packed them for disabled vets at home . . . .

In the battle between oleander and dahlia
in this way in the perfection of Time
Coach has asked me to darken his ashes
with Iwo Jima's volcanic sand
and scatter the mixture, half over his wife's grave—
she who wept with his fear—half in the sea . . . .

Today, Coach walks in elegy above his cellar.
In the synaptic concussions of his daydream, we hear . . .
but no one can listen there except dead friends from photos
of fifty years before. Rocket trucks liquid as plasma,
it may be, weeping solid as bullets, time's divisions un-
raveling to Time's seamless and deathless will;

meanwhile, below ground, in case, cold keeps his ammo.
Which of us would question him, or them,
given the simple faith of dahlia in full beauty and attack?
Spring spirals, never-arriving until, by way of a soldier's valor,
it will. His seasons return, commodious black,
perpetual witness with this flower.

The Streetcar: August 6, 1945

For several hours just after the atomic bombing of Hiroshima,
    a professional photographer,

Yoshito Matsushige, wandered the city, taking many pictures,
    not taking many others,

as when he walked up to & looked inside a streetcar jammed
    with dead passengers.

"They were all in normal positions," Yoshito said, "holding
    onto straps, sitting

"or standing still, just as they were before the bomb went off.
    Except that all

"leaned in the same direction—away from the blast. And all
    were burned black,

"a reddish black, and they were stiff." Yoshito put one foot
    up on the streetcar,

raised & focused his camera, fingered the shutter, but
    did not take this picture . . . .

This streetcar with its stiff reddish-black & leaning passengers
    now travels our city,

stops & starts at crossings for our relentless traffic. Behind
    the dutiful driver,

no one is going shopping, or visiting old parents, or working figures
    on an abacus,

or remembering a poem by an ancient master. We must not question
    or detain them, must not

stop this streetcar with our ideas in order to accept or understand,
    or to take their picture.

A Poetics of Hiroshima

Imperial Air Force pilot Sachio Ashida, unable
to fly over the burning city to report
to his superiors what had happened to it,
landed his plane, borrowed a bicycle,
& pedaled into it. He'd remember
a woman in front of her smoldering home,
a bucket on her arm. Inside the bucket
was a baby's head. The woman's daughter
had been killed when the bomb fell.

This is atrocity. You've just now descended
from a stanza wherein a baby's head—
were its eyes open or closed?—was carried
in a bucket by her mother.
An Imperial Air Force pilot stopped his bike
in front of what had been her home.
I've wanted us to breathe ashes & smoke,
but we cannot. This, too, is atrocity.

What's true for me is probably true for you:
I'm tired of trying to remember this.
Somewhere in Hiroshima the baby's head
is dreaming, wordlessly. No, it is not—this, too,
is atrocity. Ashida went on
to live a long life. He felt the swing & weight
of that bucket on his arm. No,
he did not. He did. He sometimes dreamed himself
pedaling backwards away
from that mother. I don't know whether
he did or not. Meanwhile,

we rave about the necessity of a jewel-center in every poem.
I've used a baby's head
in a bucket on her mother's arm. Whether
this is art, or in the hands of a master could be, or whether
art is atrocity, or not, I'm sick of being
or trying to be, part of it, me

with my weak auxiliary verbs which vitiate
the jewel-center, me
with my passives, my compromised stanzaic integrity,
my use of the ambiguous "this"
which is atrocity. No, it is not. It is.

For years my high school coach visited my home
with dahlias in a bucket,
big red-purple & blue-purple heads
my wife & I floated in bowls on our tables.
Have I no shame? This, too, this story
that evokes another, this narrative rhyme, this sweet
concatenation of metaphor,
is atrocity. Coach fought on Iwo Jima
for ten days before & ten days after
the flag-raising on Mount Suribachi.
He returned there fifty years later, brought me
a babyfood jar half-filled
with black sand from one volcanic blood-
soaked beach. He did. But at Marine reunions,
he couldn't locate any of his buddies
from his first outfit. No, he could not.
He once laid out on my desk aerial photos of runways
the Japanese used to "wreak havoc"—his words—
& said that hundreds of thousands of GIs would have died
if HST had not given the order.
As a participant in necessary atrocity, I agreed.
I still agree. But it doesn't matter if I agree—
what matters is whether poetry itself agrees. Incidentally,
Ashida was in training to become
a divine wind, a kamikaze.
Incidentally, in later decades Ashida himself came to agree
in the bombing of Hiroshima as necessity.
He did. But it doesn't matter if even Ashida agreed.
What matters is whether the human heart agrees.
What matters is whether art will ever agree . . . .

1945. I was almost five. Col. Tibbetts named
our *Enola Gay* for his mother.
The 6th of August. Our bomb "Little Boy" mushroomed

with the force of 15 kilotons of TNT.
"A harnessing of the basic power of the universe," said HST,
as though the universe were our plowhorse.
In the woman's home, her daughter was beheaded.
I don't know if Ashida learned exactly how,
though we & the art of atrocity would like to know.
In any case, what could this mother do?
She lifted her daughter's head. She laid it
in the aforementioned jewel-center.
She was not thinking of the basic power of the universe.
Did she place oleander blossoms on her baby's face?
Did she enfold her daughter's head in silk, which rhymes with *bucket*,
& *sick*, & *volcanic*, & *wreak havoc*? ...

Ashida attained the highest black belt, went on
to coach the American Olympic judo team.
He did. I spoke with his daughter
at an event where I received a poetry prize,
a check for a thousand George Washingtons
& an etched glass compote
for a book on the Shoah. I said I once heard her father
lecture on Zen—the moon in the river,
river flowing by that is the world with its agonies
while Moon remains in one place,
steadfast despite atrocity.
I remember that she seemed at ease,
she who had known her father
as I could never.

While teaching at the University of Hawaii,
I visited Pearl Harbor three times, launched out to the memorial
above the *Arizona*. Below us, the tomb
rusted away—a thousand sailors,
average age nineteen—for nature, too, is atrocity,
atoms transformed within it, even memory.
We tourists, some Japanese, watched minnows
nibble at our leis.
I knelt at a rail under a Japanese officer with a sword.
No, I did not. This was my dream.
But now there are too many stories for poetic safety,

for stanzaic integrity—woman & daughter,
Ashida at his lecture, my high school coach carrying heads
of dahlias grown from bulbs
he'd kept in burlap to overwinter in his cellar,
even persona Heyen at Pearl Harbor
above the rusting & decalcifying battleship that still breathed
bubbles of oil that still
iridized the Pacific swells as jewel-centers iridesce
our most anthologized villanelles . . . .

A bombing survivor said, "it's like when you burn
a fish on the grill."

Janusz Korczak, who died with his school children at Treblinka, wrote
that in his sleep he saw "One dead child
in a bucket,
another skinned, lying on boards in the mortuary,
clearly still breathing." . . .

I end my sixth line above with the word "home."
My first draft called it the woman's "house," but *home*
evokes satisfaction, *mmm*, a baby's
contentment at the breast, the atrocity
of irony, & *home* hears itself in *arm,* & *bomb,* & *blossom,*
& looks forward to *shame* & *tomb.*
I cannot tell a lie.
Apparently, I am not so disgusted with atrocity
as I'd claimed to be—my atoms
do not cohere against detonation, . . . but now time has come—listen
to the *mmm* in *time* & *come*—for closure,
as, out of the azure,

into the syntax of Hiroshima, "Little Boy" plunges—
I've centered this poem both to mushroom
& crumble its edges—
& "Fat Man," 21 kilotons of TNT,
will devastate Nagasaki. What is your history? Please don't leave
without telling me. Believe me,
I'm grateful for your enabling complicity.
I know by now you've heard my elegiac ē.
I hope your exiled mind has bucketed its breath.

I seek to compose intellectual melody.
I fuse my fear with the idea of the holy.
This is St. John's *cloud of unknowing* in me.
This is the Tao of affliction in me.
Don't try telling me my poetry is not both
beguiling & ugly.
Please help me integrate my own split psyche.

"There was no escape except to the river," a survivor said,
but the river thronged with bodies.
Black rain started falling, covering everything the survivors said.

I have no faith except in the half-life of atrocity.
I seek radiation's rhythmic sublime.
I have no faith except in poetry.
I seek the nebulous ends of time.
This is the aria those cities have made of me.
I hope my centered lines retain their integrity.
I trust that this poem will candle me.
I have no faith except in beauty.

Shoah Train: Spring Coda

This isn't blood in my pen, or semen, or venom,
not mercury or coal soot mixed with saliva,

but it's liquid, it's that same catbird's song of the dead,
isn't it not, its remembering, its *listening,* as if

the rabbi's son were still reciting, as if somewhere
in the psalms, if he could only come to it,

their lives might still be saved, as if the catbird's voice
could someday rasp something like this.

Soap

1.
Elizabeth Custer heard the Lakota story of an old woman
who'd cook soup for visitors, corn & leeks & beans
& meat simmering luscious smells, then lift open

her skull, pinch out a bit of brain, & stir it in.
Just one spoonful killed, & she killed countless.
For countless moons, she lived on & on, savaged

& boiled her victims, buried their bones in her garden,
until a child suspected her, escaped & revealed her,
at which point she disappeared into legend, as here.

2.
I don't know how beautiful that witch was, but Irma Grese,
of Auschwitz & later Belsen, was by all accounts beautiful,
slim & blond with pouting lips that even some victims

swooned for—Grese, sadistic guard, inhuman or metahuman,
kicked, broke ribs, blinded, deafened, defiled,
as though the Lakota demon had been born again,

this time not operating subtly & alone on the prairie,
but within a system of deployment centers & death camps
wherein even god gave up his word in shame at our 20th century.

3.
& consider Maria Mandel, *SS*, Auschwitz, glad
to fulfill her duties to the Reich, to lead children to the gas.
She caressed the cutest to calm them, but at the same time

teased them into chambers she believed their Palestine—
the children, she was sure, were & would be vermin.
At war's end, her great regret was the program's cessation.

Mandel is almond in German, the smell of this woman
lingering in the history of atrocity like the smell of almond
emanating from corpses from injections of cyanide.

4.
& consider lethally seductive Lieutenant Podust
prowling her web during the early 1980s as the Soviet Union,
in its virulent death throes, rewarded such as she

to perfect skills to turn those who said *No* into animals.
Look into Irina Ratushinskaya's prison memoir *Gray*
Is the Color of Hope, hundreds of pages of suffering by way

of twisted Podust & her superiors who tried to obliterate
Irina's poetry (sometimes scratched with a burnt match on bars
of ersatz soap, memorized, washed off, smuggled out to survive).

Rose

I had a friend who planned to become
a dead poet.
It wasn't easy, but he worked at it
until it

became him & he it, lungs & heart
& Rilkean
attar of swoon in his oxygen tubes.
I loved him,

it wasn't easy, but I worked at it
until it
did seem, didn't it, that dying spring,
a kind of song

between us, as if I might, after all, not
survive him.
Rainer Maria writes long letters
from his castles,

I hope my friend can still receive them,
though I cannot,
though an occasional streaked blossom still
seems to fall.

Fledgling

I then listened to a catbird about everything
under the shade. The catbird mewed
sound sequences close to singing,
but not song, unless song remains, at best,
arhythmic melody; unless melody remains,
at best, only rents & fragments, only
the gasped ingestion of *Zyklon B* . . . .

From here, this evening, I sense her nesting
in my forehead. Any surviving baby
will soon be fledgling twirling among
honeysuckle leaves & berries,
as she does, when she is not singing,
or not lisping sounds that once were song.
We might hear such remembering

as is possible from black & gray smoke filtering
into trees that still host them every spring,
& will, except they do not seem nearly
as confident as sometimes my deluded meanings
used to be, it may be. Whoever you are,
I write you to revise me in the aftertime
for hearing what was never the catbird's song.

Blueberries Album

1.
A bucket of previously unrecorded black & white preliberation Auschwitz photos has been uncovered. I've tasted some of them online. They are of the *SS* & their *Helferinnen*, the female auxiliary. It seems that all these personages are having a good time, relaxing from their duties.

2.
A July 11, 1944 snapshot shows a group of eleven *Helferinnen* sitting on a railing on an outdoor deck. They are with officer Karl Höcker. They have just now finished eating their bowls of blueberries.

3.
During my boyhood, wild blueberries grew in abundance along the sand-edged tar roads in Nesconset in the center of Long Island. Once in a while, I'd stop my bike for a handful on a summer day. My mind wants to go back to those days now.

4.
Once, hiding from a friend, I knelt in a thicket of blueberries & was stung by a bumblebee. I'd often been stung by yellowjackets, & once by a hornet, but this bumblebee sting—well, while I'm thinking of it now, my left temple buzzes a little where the bee got me about 55 years ago. No kidding: nerves between cheekbone & ear remember that yellow & black & reddish-pink—the flowers of the blueberry are reddish-pink—jolt.

5.
This photo from Raul Hilberg's *The Destruction of the European Jews*: "The corpses were pink in color, with green spots." These were the gassing victims at Auschwitz.

6.
I once made ink from crushed blueberries, scratched some words with it with a quill pen.

7.
The women are wearing their uniforms of white blouses & pleated knee-length skirts. These women all maintain very full hair.

8.
I don't remember what words I might have written to try out my blueberry ink. Maybe I wrote my name, too. Is a name a word?

9.

These women are without exception smiling, except for one who holds her bowl upside down. She is frowning to show that she is so sad, so *traurig* that her berries are all gone. O how she'd like to have another portion of the sweet delicious fruit. O she's just a child in a fairy tale: won't somebody please refill her bowl with more of the luscious little blue eyes?

10.

Once in a while I'd pick a jelly jar of the wild berries & take them home to my mother who liked to sugar them & pour milk over them & spoon a few at a time into her mouth. Back then, my mother was a big woman with big hair. She looked very much like a composite of the female auxiliary.

11.

The other women are showing their empty bowls, showing that they have been good little girls & have finished their healthy berries. Mama & Papa will be so pleased.

12.

My mother hated/hates the Jews, blamed/blames the war on them.

13.

In the photo, another man is relaxing in a deck chair in front of the women & Höcker, the back of his head to the camera. We know what is in this head. All in the photo know, too, of course, what has been going on in their camp, what they themselves have been doing. On this particular July day, only 150 or so prisoners are being murdered, but from February 1942 to November 1944 1,000,000 Jews were victims here, & the time of this photo is the time of the arrival at the camp of the Hungarian Jews. The United States Holocaust Memorial Museum timeline reads, in part: "May 16, 1944: Following the German occupation of Hungary, the first transports of Hungarian Jews began arriving in Auschwitz-Birkenau. Nearly 440,000 Hungarian Jews will be deported from Hungary, most of them to Auschwitz, by July 1944. The majority of deportees will be taken directly to the gas chambers or shot."

14.

It wasn't easy to kill thousands of men, women, children at a time, but the *SS* / *Helferinnen* / various kapos worked long hours to accomplish this harvest that was so delectable to so many of them, especially the sadists among them.

15.

I don't think I ever did, & I still don't especially enjoy the taste of blueberries, certainly not as much as the taste of peaches, grapes, pears, apples, watermelon, yes, & oranges, yes & cherries, yes. Blueberries possess something of the miasmal fen and/or grave, &, when fully ripe, their texture is a combination of suppurating gauze & pond muck.

16.

There must have been caches of Hungarian blueberries in the freight cars. Some children must have been pacified with them. There must have been blueberry vomit & blueberry diarrhea.

17.

It's hard to tell from the photos what time of day it is—maybe mid- or late-afternoon. Maybe, in an hour or two, these personages will all have coffee & an assortment of cakes & ices. & what is in store for them this very evening? There is an air of flirtation in this & other photos.

18.

My mother was born in Bremerhaven on the day WWI started, August 1, 1914. As I write, she is 93, resident in a nursing home just a few miles away from me here in western New York State. Today I asked her if the blueberries in Germany were the same kind as those that grew on the Island, for there are many species. Yes, she said, exactly the same, no question about it. She said that she & her several sisters & her brother would pick them, that her mother would boil them into syrup for pancakes, & also mix them into the batter. She said that her father loved these pancakes, that she herself could still smell them as they sizzled into firmness in her mother's black iron skillets.

19.

The skin of the ripest Nesconset blueberries was not shiny, but smoky, hazy.

20.

How fierce & tough my mother is. She does not want ever to die. She is now angrily recovering from surgery after a second broken hip. She is a force of nature. As long as she is alive, all those Jews are dead, & will stay dead.

21.

My mother said that they were called *Bickberen*. She spelled the word out: B-I-C-K-B-E-R-E-N. But I can't find such a word in my English-German dictionary. Blueberries are identified as *Blaubeere* or *Heidelbeere*. *Blau* is blue, of course; the *Heidel* might go to heather/moor/heath.

22.

The blueberries disappeared from Nesconset roadsides during about the time I went to high school & college. Lawns were planted, & the mauves of lilacs—Walt Whitman's memory bloom—& the yellows of forsythia bushes, & the pinks of ornamental trees as the Suffolk County building boom heightened.

23.

My herbalist says that the leaves & berries of this low shrub are to be mixed a teaspoonful to a cup of boiling water, one or two cups to be imbibed each day, that this is "of great value in diarrhea."

24.

The leaves & flowers of this plant may be useful as an astringent. My dictionary says that an astringent is "a substance that constricts the tissues or canals of the body, thereby diminishing discharges, as of mucus or blood." But there was not enough astringent in the cattle cars to stanch all the discharges of mucus & blood, urine & watery feces. There was not enough in Europe. There is not now enough astringent in the cosmos to stanch the discharges from the Shoah transports.

25.

Often, thinking about things, we do not want to think about them, but it's time now to begin to think, at least to begin to think about beginning to think about thinking, I think.

26.

In the *Kabbalah*, colors commence with blue. Blue is the first to emerge from black. Blue opens & releases black. I cannot not think about this, but my mind can neither encircle nor penetrate this blueberry poetry.

27.

In our Nesconset cellar, my mother submerged white shirts & blouses & socks in a basin of bluing water.

28.

We can't know everything. Maybe one of these women was in emotional & spiritual turmoil, hated herself & her place here, did not brutalize the condemned, could not sleep, forced herself to smile for this photo.

29.

A friend of mine said that once upon a time in the Adirondacks he was alone, picking blueberries, when he heard a rustle in the bushes. A black bear cub emerged. Guess what fearful thought, at that moment, came blueberrying into his mind.

30.

My encyclopaedia says that these days Auschwitz is a center of communications where five railway lines meet.

31.

There would have been no way to escape from the mother bear's jaws.

32.

Blueberry flowers bear five dark blue or black seeds.

33.

Blueberry bushes thrive in acidic soils. But what does my stomach ache matter? What do these photos matter?

34.

Go backward in time from when the color blue first appears in the bush's white berries. Halve that first blue &, however pale, there is still some slight tinge or essence of blue. Halve this slight blue again, & again, & according to the law of infinite divisibility, there is still some blue that will always be there, that was there from the beginning.

35.

Speaking of human nature: think of the *SS* man who, while drowning a newborn baby under a faucet sang, "There you go, little Moses, down the stream.". . . But, no, this might not have been his innate nature. But think of him, his education. Deal with him.

36.

The wild blueberries were fairly small. *Zyklon B* pellets were a half to a third the size of the berries the *SS* consumed that day; they were porous, chalky, with a slight bluish tinge. *Zyklon B* deteriorated fairly quickly, like blueberries. Hurry, before it is too late, let us refill the bowls of Höcker & these women, this time with those pellets. But then, who would we be?

37.

I've known from my beginnings that I'll have completed this album only when it can sustain itself on its own blueberries, only when it does not sicken itself. Or do I have this the wrong way around?

38.

Höcker & the women are having a wonderful time, it appears. He is hip to hip with them, as I am, our female auxiliaries, my muses, my blueberries.

The Carriages

It's one thing to hear of 200,000 children murdered
at Auschwitz; another, as two witnesses testified,
that empty baby carriages were pushed in rows of five
to the railroad station, taking long & long to pass by.

No doubt some *Kinderwagen* were poor & plain,
others of the finest lacquered wicker & satin.
No matter. What matters within this vacuum
teethes the human scream we cannot fathom.

We will not, will we, again, in time,
mother so much absence? Always, now,
those children must remain behind
as carriages form lines of obscene sound.

The Killers

As I dream, a gas chamber forms.
Light awakens inside it.
Otherwise, that space is empty.
Its doors swing shut.

Gas drops in.
The gas fills the chamber.
The light is being gassed.
The killers are killing the light.

The Light

The fact is that there occurred discussions among officers
as to whether it would be best
during gassings

to leave lights on in the chambers or turn them off.
I don't know what,
in the end—

for efficiency or for the sensibilities of the . . . facilitators
was decided,
or if,

in fact, a consistent policy existed. In the end,
the insensate entangled innocent
were dragged out

into the Aryan light of the 1940s into which
I was issued from the womb
of a Jew-hater

into the light of gold teeth at this zenith of human time.
The doors open. Dead light
reveals me.

from

Hiroshima Suite

(2012)

Preface

The first four lyrics of William Heyen's *Hiroshima Suite,* interesting as they are as they introduce two of the book's main characters, are just asymmetrical purchase, but then, as he has written elsewhere, "the moment of the poem arrives," & it arrives here in waves of 15-line meditative cerebrations that refract, as art must, "the agonies [that] encandle us."

Here they are, then: Mrs. Aoyama who, at Point Zero, has less than no time to realize anything of what happens when Little Boy detonates; & heroic Mr. Tanimoto who ferries the living dead toward green across Hiroshima's Ota River. To the poet, too, a fish appears—a blunt-headed witness creature as aura-drenched as any in our literature—& a bamboo pole with multitudinous eyes, & a stowaway mouse. & you. & Heyen's often double-negative & triple-negative compromised song as the *Enola Gay,* doesn't it never not, accomplishes its design. Its engines keep revving in the radiated mnemonic memorial water that passes through the fish's gills. "Even the Buddha's dilemma / is how not to drown in it as he sips moon from that water."

I invite you to allow this *Hiroshima Suite*—which the poet seems to have heard all at once in one non-linear audition—to intone for you until, within the "transluminous horror" of August 6, 1945, we are never not whole again but are, at the same time, in Robert Frost's phrase, "beyond confusion."

Edwina Seaver
Rome / 2012

Kimono

Even though in a minute or two she will cease to exist,
we are glad to know about Mrs. Aoyama.
Mrs. Aoyama happened to be pretty much exactly
right below detonation point zero in Hiroshima.
Hers was perhaps the fastest death in history,
human or otherwise: before even one nerve cell
could sense danger, before any scintillation of brain
intuited her into awareness, Mrs. Aoyama vanished
as though she had never been .... And we?:
we'll remember this woman as the very definition
of translation, from the here to the gone ....
Let us picture her before she vanishes into then.
Let us remember that Mrs. Aoyama experienced no pain.

The Park

Even as firestorm spread, Kyoshi Tanimoto found a boat
        on a branch of the Ota River.
Before borrowing it, he begged pardon of the several burned dead
        who'd been working on or near it—
he told them he required the boat for others who, unlike them,
        were still extant. Thus it came to pass
that Tanimoto ferried survivors across the river to a park where many,
        in fact, would soon expire. For some reason,
I enjoy saying his trochaic surname, *Tanimoto, Tanimoto,*
        until it mushrooms—forgive my metaphor—
as names & dates do: *Tanimoto,* August 6, 1945 ....

His ferry held ten or twelve, we don't know exactly
        the number of his crossings,
nor did this not never happen before, hasn't it not?
        Now we of the present seize time

to join him among the ten or twelve, nor will our presence exclude
        even one other victim, for in our mnemonic state
we occupy only particles of space. *Tanimoto*, we'll call,
        as we run toward him, *take us with you,*
we've nowhere else to hope for except the park with its trees . . .

but Tanimoto cannot hear us, but no matter, there's no time even
        to wake from this rhythmic nightmare, isn't there?
But now, despite everything, he turns toward us & beckons us
        to breathe such history as enlightens us. Our boat
casts off. What's not to trust about ferryman Tanimoto?

Bamboo Pole

If we forget about Mr. Tanimoto for a long time,
if then for no conscious reason he appears again,
ferrying traumatized exiles to a park,
what is our relationship with him, & them, ex-
cept that of dreamer to dream ex-
cept that *they* awaken,

& not us? Just where are you, right now,
Mr. Tanimoto, you with your bamboo pole
by which we cross between near & far shores?
Sir, Grandfather Mnemonic, *Tanimoto*, you wax
stronger, measure by measure, as the spreading fire-
storm reddens your black hair.

L: The Mirror

I
Another refracted detail to reveal:
he parted his hair neatly down the middle.
That part might remind us of the bamboo pole
which might remind us of river water & April,
in Hiroshima or elsewhere, before Little Boy befell,
but when the bomb detonated, Hiroshima became horizontal.

II
Earlier that morning, it is more than probable
that Mr. Tanimoto parted his hair down the middle,
as always. Mr. Tanimoto's segmented bamboo pole
may now be thought of as . . . elemental . . . primordial.
August 6, 1945. Early morning. A man wets his full
head of hair & parts it, just so, down the middle.

The Fish

I don't know why I keep seeing a fish accompanying Tanimoto
        on his trips forth & back across the river.
He doesn't notice it, but keeps to his navigation,
        nor do his passengers see the gold-finned one
now in their wake, now at their prow, now beneath them.
        What can I do with its blunt forehead that comes knocking
into me no matter where I am or what doing ex-
        cept not to name it, for naming presumes?
Look, just now, did you see the fish almost struck
        as Tanimoto shoved his bamboo pole into the water?
There it is, again, at the point of refraction, itself
        divided, part black, part gold, broken
but whole, able to keep swimming, able to breathe.
        Tanimoto, Tanimoto, it will not abandon you, or me,
this moving cloud, this blunt beauty, this spirit in the water.

The Fish

The flash x-rayed a fish in the river.
       If we could have seen, we'd have seen every bone,
every organ, at that instant, including its heart.
       At that instant, enlightenment became a shadow in it.
For a while, it swam aimlessly, sometimes among others,
       sometimes alone, sometimes in open water, sometimes
within a reflection of trees along the river's bank.
       Then it saw the shadow of the boat we know,
Tanimoto's, & in its new state of awareness,
       attached itself to Tanimoto's labor, if only
to be there, helplessly, but, yes, to be there. *Whoosh*—
       Tanimoto's pole almost impales it, but doesn't.
It can still swim. It keeps swimming. Nothing
       but death will keep it from shadowing his boat.
Nothing will never not keep Tanimoto from not seeing it.

The Question

To reprise the immediate aftermath of the flash
       with Mr. Tanimoto: he threw himself
between rocks in a garden in case these might shield him
       from whatever it was that had just happened.
He looked up into what seemed to be twilight this morning.
       He might have wondered: Is it possible
for God to create a rock so heavy that He himself
       cannot lift it? Tanimoto plunged for cover,
we wish we could just leave him there until he awakens
       from the weapon that disarms us, but we cannot,
will never negate not. He stood up from those rocks,
       climbed a hill, looked down into his miasmal city,
thought of his family, his home, his parishoners.
       He could not move those rocks nor never
not try to ferry them with us all the way to here.

Kimonos

A woman ran from the city with a koi burned
       into her chest from the pattern on her kimono.
Tanimoto saw her, he saw the fish, the fish
       swam downward toward her navel
in the color of blood mixed with pus.
       This fish had been swimming in silk in en-
foldings of shadowy water. Now in agony—no
       it was not, it was not a species of living fish,
it felt no pain—it moved toward & past Tanimoto,
       its gills clogged with char & the woman's fat.
It could not breathe even if it had to.
       It could not be researched or watercolored.
Its blackened fins crusted toward & into Tanimoto
       in a nightmare of women whose kimonos
transferred fish & flowers & dragonflies from fire to flesh.

The End

If at all possible I'd rather not stop talking about Mr. Tanimoto,
       his parted black hair, his bamboo pole,
& the fish that I imagine as accompanying us, in Time,
       forth & back across the river. It is not that
to stop talking would be to cease remembering. It is not that
       to stop talking would be to practice resignation.
It is just that if I stopped talking I might be left to see
       with all these x-rayed eyes at the moment of the flash.
I need to keep talking until the bomb, that *tremendum*,
       if it ever not will never, drinks back into itself
the unleashed light. If I do not never cease not talking,
       Enola Gay will be sailing toward but not reach the city.
But now I tell myself to desist. I close my mouth,
       but cannot not think or never not need to scream.

The Poem

Its eyes gleam, it scurries, you know what it is.
　　　　It made its nest in rags under canvas in the bow
under fishing gear & a wire cage in need of repair.
　　　　& now it travels forth & back with Tanimoto,
afraid not nor even to stay just where it is or
　　　　venture out into the strange darkening morning
to sniff the air & to see nor never sense in the same way
　　　　such water. How can we not just concentrate
our words on it, the little gray bewhiskered creature
　　　　whose every cell is now suffused with fear?
Tanimoto, this entity is never not the very least
　　　　of your passengers nor will it ever not need
to reach the park, so will you not discover some way
　　　　to leave it there or will this vital one itself
smell a green future of grass & trees, & somehow disembark?

Gills & Scales

No one knows when the fish wouldn't stop gilling
　　　　the gruesome flesh-tinged water,
but the water did clear unless we remember, & who
　　　　doesn't not desire to remember unless
it's you, & it might be me, & it might or might not be
　　　　Tanimoto in his hereafter, or Aioyama
during her incomprehensible fusion with atoms.
　　　　Those gills kept straining, keep oxygenating,
into the present & future tenses, like hell they do,
　　　　even when the fish sleeps in its riverbank cave,
even while you & I travel into the unimaginable,
　　　　or at least toward it a little ways,
maybe along one frilled gill, maybe within one scale bend-
　　　　ing such light as a contact lens bends
our cosmos, now look, look, the whole fish becoming lens!

After Pearl Harbor

When he was through with it Tanimoto's bamboo pole
      found itself afloat there where
the wounded flung themselves in their strips of burnt flesh
      into the water. If it is true as some say
that bamboo has eyes, Tanimoto's pole saw enough
      for all of us those days, so we'll let it be.
My experience with bamboo takes you, my poem,
      on a tour to Hawaii's fecundity where
thick stalks grew in a lagoon in organ-pipe clumps
      twenty-thirty feet high. When my wife & I ex-
ited the van, we got behind a haole who lit a cigarette,
      the path was narrow, we had to follow his smoke
through ferns & flowers to where the bamboo flourished.
      I now know I intimated the mind & soul of Tanimoto.
When the tour group left, my wife & I were last to follow.

Beauty

& if it was/is infinitely worse than this assymetrical suite has even
      not never ventured to not say now or ever,
I may be excused by Tanimoto who kept telling himself,
      These are human beings, as he lifted the slough-
skinned bodies into his boat. Two sisters were standing
      like stalks of charred bamboo in the river,
they were cold on this our first post-atomic evening, the younger
      suffered terribly as the salt water ex-
coriated her, she shivered with cold & pain until
      dead. In *Hiroshima Forever*
Michael Perlman says that Tanimoto as he lifted slimy bodies
      was "in touch with inhuman dread."
Tanimoto touched them he had to touch them he lifted them he
      had to never *not* touch them didn't he not?
The atrocity of his inhuman dread. The beauty of Tanimoto.

Candles

Mrs. Aoyama & Mr. Tanimoto of Hiroshima,
     my old friends for weeks now, they
of the flash & firestorm, the one instantly translated,
     the other ferrying himself & traumatized others
across the water of Time into my own time—
     I begin already to miss them, do I?
I presume to say that she was a good woman, he
     a man who could be trusted to spend his last strength
poling us to where trees & lawn & gardens receive
     ash & black rain but, nevertheless, survive—
root hairs strengthen & take deeper hold when wind
     or atomic shock, from bearable distance,
trembles them. I've not seen a photo of either one,
     if a photo of her exists, but have their x-rays
in me. These two in their lives in that city did

not know one another, but do know one another now
     by way of such mnemonics as we might hear
as we, dare I say it, sing them? There she is, Mrs. Aoyama,
     doing what she's doing when she disappears
without knowledge of cause & effect. There he is,
     Mr. Tanimoto, who at first thinks
an earthquake has shuddered Hiroshima & caused fires,
     but then realizes, does he, that God is not to blame
for this which has happened. Leave me, stay with me,
     intercede no never not for me, for us,
you two & the others who in their instantaneous disappearance
     or prolonged agonies encandle us.
We do confess that history x-rays us as we
     repeat to ourselves, as we ready ourselves
for our own sleep among its shadows, *Aoyama, Tanimoto.*

In The Beginning

Let us consider, then, a human being, Mrs. Aoyama,
      at the trillisecond of her vanishing,
her translation into such infinitesimal elements
      that we might as well identify this new estate of hers
as primordial—even her eyeglasses were suddenly
      not there by which we might see,
her shoes by which we might walk a few steps into her,
      her teeth by which we might chew her genre;
in fact, history, too, at Mrs. Aoyama's *trump l'oil*,
      fused with the cosmic mind
which is our mind: mind how as we consider Point Zero,
      its flash & power, its transluminous horror,
we still divide us from then when, in point of fact—
      isn't the ever not never *not* for us to say?—
Mrs. Aoyama's body reprises the Milky Way.

Noon

I dream my severed leg kicks out at Mr. Tanimoto.
      It is one passenger. Next to it,
my spine has its place, & behind it my heart,
      & next to my heart what is it, it must be
my skull, that smoldering shape which eschews integration.
      Tanimoto's boat moves not at all,
but the river passes beneath us. He stands at the prow
      with his pole, he stands astern with his pole,
he is refracted, a gold-finned fish swims abreast,
      a turtle with burning carapace keeps the fish company,
these creatures are my dream's only color, I cannot
      see that shore to which Mr. Tanimoto prays.
I hear his intoning voice, a murmur, he asks to awaken
      from this nightmare, but his passengers
& the swimming creatures know better, blur & siren.

The Fish

About which I might or might not have been confused, or lying.
     Gold-finned but not a goldfish,
not a koi. Blunt-headed, bewhiskered,
     reminding us of a Mississippi channel catfish,
behemoth nosing beneath riverbank logs & into dens,
     but this one keeping Mr. Tanimoto faithful company
as he poles the stricken to the other shore, leaves them there,
     & returns for others, & makes his way across river again,
is not American. It is not nor Japanese. This one
     is the witness fish sent from the father, sent from
the father of the atom, no it is not, no, this is silly,
     the quizzical fish lies & lies, what does it think it is,
what does it eat, how does it keep its strength,
     what do its gills smell in that flashed river flowing
from the atom, what do its eyes make of bamboo

stabbing refracted lines down past it into silt
     that clouds & settles, what does it make
of the murky light of its father & the inedible ash
     that sifts past it now, what is its essence about which
I keep asking, help me, my mnemonic, my appositive father,
     to sleep as the fish had been sleeping all its life
before the bombs? It awoke from the rocks. It swam
     out into the river. It found the shadow
of Mr. Tanimoto's boat. Its gold fins flashed
     beneath that shadow. In its own way it read
every broken human word Mr. Tanimoto stabbed into the water.
     It wanted nothing, it kept swimming, the ferryman
worked hard, it was all he could do, he lifted, he assisted,
     he washed blood & fat from his hands in the river,
he kept on. The fish, that night, rested. It readied itself.

Mind

I was thinking about Mrs. Aoyama again when
       I backed my car into a grocery cart.
I didn't hit it hard, but did hit it. The cart had rolled
       from where someone had left it in a parking space,
so it was only half my fault, I was distracted, & all that.
       At the moment of inconsequential impact,
the Mrs. Aoyama in my mind lived in the millisecond
       just before she disappeared. She wasn't sure
whether or not she'd heard the plane, which was backing away
       after dropping that pumpkin,
as one commentator later phrased it. She wasn't sure
       whether or not she'd . . . at that instant I heard
the cart I'd hit go down with a metallic clang.
       Whatever it was I'd had in mind for Mrs. Aoyama
always again never to be unsure about, she vanished.

Change, Please

Mr. Tanimoto charged each passenger the equivalent
       of two U.S. dollars for his or her one-way trip.
Even the ones whose wallets had been burned from their persons,
       the ones whose kimonos were saturated with fat,
had to cough up the dough or they were going nowhere.
       On each trip, he netted about twenty U.S. dollars,
which was good money, in fact great money at the time, but,
       truth be told, he was pissed that no one wanted
to ferry with him from the other side back to where
       he'd stolen the boat (speak about low overhead!) . . . .
If truth be told, we & Mr. Tanimoto could use a laugh,
       & he is not devoid of humor despite all he suffered,
despite all they all suffered. Did you hear the one about the blonde
       painted on the bomb?—she thought she'd had
her first orgasm. But too much is lost in translation.

Poetry

I think I am not done with them yet,
        they are tattoos on me, in me—the bamboo pole,
the boat borrowed from the dead, the park, the river
        within which that fish, or turtle, or both of them
are atomic presences, &, of course, the two who,
        so far as I know, were never together until
that cataclysm in Hiroshima, or maybe not never,
        or are they, now, by way of my exegesis?
In any case, what possible use do I serve ex-
        cept insofar as their mnemonic nature
enables me to keep seeking them? Mrs. *Aoyama*, Mr. *Tanimoto*,
        I thank you for what you've given me—you,
ferryman, from your psychic agony, & you, woman,
        who passed without pain or knowledge from Hiroshima
to here. Was/is there anything I could/can do for you?

Faith

A child holding her own eye in her open palm,
        & she wondering if it can still see though she can-
not see herself with it, & we wondering as we read of this
        if that organ can see us—no, we are not serious,
we know her Hiroshima eye is not really looking at us,
        is it, should it, must it, did it, will it,
for what have we to do with her? After all, the gold-
        finned fish is there in place of us,
its whiskers cursive in the current, the moon in the river
        remains in one place under breastbone, yes,
while the misery of the world flows by but is inter-
        sected now by Mr. Tanimoto's boat. The eye
in the daughter's open hand is seeking him,
        there he is, returning from the far shore—
he'll know what to do with her wild pupil & watercolored iris.

Direction

You're now almost halfway across the river, listener,
    on one of Mr. Tanimoto's trips. Around you,
some are in shock, some groan, one man vomits,
    a woman's face is seared blind, the boat
refracts forward as if by force of grunts & cries. Over there,
    the park exists as in a dream: once reached,
it might retract what happened, couldn't it not,
    is happening now. Birds seem to suffer
from the same illusion, flying in toward green.
    You guess the huge annual Hiroshima garden show
is canceled. You grimace at yourself, your esophagas & sternum
    seem reversed, something is happening in the forehead
of your cave. The ferryman pushes on, thrust
    by thrust of his pole into the still-liquid water
moving east, or is it west, or both, or somewhere neither.

The Fish

Never mind my saying that Mr. Tanimoto never saw
    the fish. He did see the underwater bullion
of its gold fins. He thought, in fact, that if his pole could
    manage to touch its blunt forehead,
he & all his passengers could awaken from this nightmare.
    But this was not to be—his pole kept being
refracted in the river, the fish kept to itself even while
    accompanying the ferryman, it bore
its atomic source into & through the water of which it was born.
    The closest anyone ever came from fathoming it, in fact,
was Mrs. Aoyama at the trillisecond of her translation,
    but even then that fish ignored her,
so determined was it to hold to its own *raison d'etre*.
    Well, then, if we are looking to place blame, let us
focus on the fish whose evolution splits the atom.

The Moon

The water. Only the flashed water. The water in the river.
      Nothing but the flowing water, not even
(shore) or (overhanging branches), just the water in
      & of the river. The water moves from Hiroshima
but stays, grayblue, browngreen, the infinite divisi-
      bilities of yellows & cherry reds all suffused
with shadow, the murmuring movement of the water.
      But since we need this, & since it is there & not there,
we allow the presence of moon in river—see
      how it stays as the water leaves Hiroshima but remains.
We remember what the moon was, before we walked on it.
      Some say a Christ can walk on water,
but this river's water cannot bear the weight of such
      a divine personage, even the Buddha's dilemma
is how not to drown in it as he sips moon from that water.

Resurrection

When the question was put to God, God created a rock
      that he himself could not lift.
Don't ask. Point Zero = paradox that exists
      in an equilibrium as though the cosmos flows
at once in all directions, as it does for Mr. Tanimoto
      poling his boat, this time, back from the far shore—
he is relieved during these return crossings as he prays,
      but relief gnaws in him like his companion,
the little gray stowaway under canvas, even though
      it's not there for him even while it is. Aloneness,
it may be—we won't presume to impose words on his thought—
      is that interim between skin that sticks to bones
& that which sloughs off & must be unceremoniously flicked
      or slung into water that receives it with such non-
chalance that maybe the dead will form from it again.

Ars Poetica

At Pearl Harbor the average age of the *Arizona* dead was nineteen,
        a thousand perished within that ship above which
I walked as though from one far shore of America to every other,
        behind funeral processions, dressed in black sheaves,
all the land a prayer shawl that could not be lifted until
        Little Boy deformed Hiroshima into inferno, & then
not even then. I for one cannot stop hating
        Mrs. Aoyama & Mr. Tanimoto for what I assume
was their assumed imperial allegiance. Let the whole
        Japanese empire vanish as that woman did, let
its emperor's skin slough off into the river of my repugnance.
        How transcend this caustic iniquity of mine?
I guard my black heart as though it were a Holocaust candle.
        I hate them, hellward, & will, but trust my poem
to be a decidedly better man than I am.

This Field

Away from the river for a while, away from the city
        to ricefields where dragonflies glint
in & out of light as though nothing had happened in Hiroshima.
        With their many-faceted eyes, the flying ones see
from all sides at once; with their ovipositors,
        they dip down to touch reeds & leaves with eggs,
& these cycles continue even while . . . but never mind
        what is happening over there beyond these fields
which still receive the sun which has not gone black,
        nor has there not any not black rain or ash rain fallen,
hasn't it not? The dragonflies seem to our senses
        to celebrate sheen, but no such thing is happening here—
they are creatures of nerve & instinct, their wings do rainbow,
        but beauty, so far as we know, does not
interest them as such . . . . But now it is time again for Tanimoto . . . .

Blossoms

Enough now. Aoyama, who disappeared, & Tanimoto,
        whose shadow crossed & recrossed that river,
need time, & we with them. Atoms dissipated
        from the flash & various vaporizations.
The 20th Century came to pass, & there were no solutions to questions
        of atrocity & beauty. What aspired to be poetry
continued to aspire, but it was no use: the blunt-headed fish
        kept thinking its way into every poet's aspirations until
thought piled on thought on thought with refracted lines
        so jagged & stupid that the art of prayer was forgotten.
God kept playing & replaying original sin or *tabula rasa*—
        have it your way, He seemed to be saying.
In Hiroshima & in Washington, D.C., cherry trees buzzed & bloomed.
        No use trying to describe all those warming scents & colors
flowing like a river that beguiles us to remember.

Generations

At the university, a stand of young bamboo writers
        grew in the far corner of the aud as, for the first time,
I read parts of this still-untyped Hiroshima suite I'd written
        for the most part in the flow of a flashed river.
They'd distanced themselves in their communal spatial language
        that seemed to say Who the fuck are you, anyway,
old man, you with your impositions, your Aoyama & Tanimoto,
        your blunt-headed fish & a mouse or rat under canvas,
shove that pole up your refracted anus, leave us alone, . . .
        but this might have been / was probably my own
shyness & paranoia—maybe they were scared,
        or I too ugly & bald for their empathy,
reminded them of every melted-down decrepit fart
        who lectured incessantly on imminent danger
from history withered ones like me had made, the violence

& gore, the heartless hatred that climaxed at Auschwitz & Hiroshima.
      In any case, I've got a strong voice,
I read to them & to the others "Kimono" & "The Park" & "Bamboo Pole,"
      then a dozen or fifteen of the fifteen-liners.
Between poems, I interjected bits & pieces from Wallace Stevens
      about poetry resisting intelligence, & from William Stafford
who said he had clues to forward motion in poetry, & from Kabir
      who said we're all looking for the great ruby,
& from a German critic who spoke of the necessity of rhythmical narcosis,
      & from JCO who mentions the semi-trance within which
we all read & write, etc., etc., these associations coming to me
      as easily as John Keats' leaves to a tree in that park
to which Mr. Tanimoto poled through neutrinos of Mrs. Aoyama
      to try to find psychic shade despite inhuman dread.
Unless I was mistaken, the young in their corner of hermetic heaven
      began to listen, & I to them, amen.

Ohmmm

I don't know what they were doing in my garden,
      or in what used to be my garden—
my wife & I haven't planted anything back there for years,
      but now use the fenced-in plot for compost,
for feeding birds, for margin for milkweed to form leaves
      then seedpods then mauve blossoms.
Yes, this was the April week when eighteen West Virginia miners ex-
      pired in an explosion of chambers & seams
where fossils come to black light & are powered
      by conveyor belts & railcars
back to the living world. This was that week, yes,
      but I lived states away from where the miners
died within geologic time, but here they were, in my garden,
      laid out, some on top of one another, cordwood, some
with raccoon-like masks, all in boots & coveralls, some

with headlamps faintly shining in the half-dark of what,
        I didn't not know, must have been my dream.
I approached them, I seemed to understand nothing,
        I heard a sound in this confusion of space & time,
the world's *ohmmm*. The miners were dead, weren't they
        not never, but when I widened my eyes
a few chests seemed to rise then decompress as though
        all the bodies were merely asleep. Then this flash
of doom & enlightenment: there, among them, Tanimoto
        kept his mouth open as if within a sentence or sound
he'd never complete. There's no correspondence,
        my garden was not his boat, isn't there not, between
the dead West Virginia miners & the inhabitants of in-
        cinerated Hiroshima within whatever sentence, or sound,
he couldn't, not never, complete.

The The

In the words of President Harry Truman the atomic bomb
        represented "a harnessing of the basic power of the universe,"
but Tanimoto, poling grievously wounded passengers across the river,
        was not thinking of absurd metaphor, of a satanic weapon
as ox or plowhorse. He was not contemplating the nature of light,
        the perversion of primal essence into ash comprised
of what had once been plant & flesh. No, we'll leave not
        Tanimoto but Mrs. Aoyama in the realm of meditation,
for she is vortex in her translation into elsewhere
        & nowhere at once. It's not horses or oxen
that she sees pulling Hiroshima toward quasar, but
        a blunt-headed fish, & not by harness but by dis-
cordant waves that radiate from its fins,
        that metric fish whose brain cannot mourn, whose eyes
see further than countless moons in countless rivers.

The Divine

God stood up in the fire. He said to Mr. Tanimoto,
    Fulfill my prophecy: ferry the wounded & dying
to greenery across the river. But here's where it gets crazy:
    Mr. Tanimoto had already done this, this was night
after the long day of transport, what in hell was God talking about,
    what dimension of time did that voice & presence inhabit,
how is prophecy what had already happened, maybe
    terror & agony are retroactive! The ferryman thought
of starting over, but from the opposite side of the river,
    carrying the same ones back again even if
into the as-yet-not-green-after-the-bomb until
    green reappeared & lives resumed & the past
were Hiroshima again. He couldn't wait to get started.
    In the middle of his sleep, he returned to his boat, told God
Tanimoto was ready, but God had become a cloud.

Spirit

As for her, at the trillisecond of her translation God
    did hear from Mrs. Aoyama. There was time,
plenty of time, time was not part of the equation
    as the woman vaporized into vacancy on earth
as if God's thought & the act itself were synchronous,
    as they are. In any case, here she is, bodiless
but somehow filling out the shape of her blue & gold kimono
    & ready to tell God a thing or two but now
there is too much light even for this eyeless woman
    who'd been minding her business in human time
until timelessly elsewhere, as here. Still, she's determined
    to ask who it is makes these decisions, in fact
she'll demand to know for her family's sake, her city's sake.
    Therefore, rest assured, we still have an able advocate
there in that dimension, & she's having our say.

Pathetic

The bamboo pole thought, thrust after thrust,
        that it was glad it was not a sensitive conductor
of light & heat. The bomb's flash was
        as of nothing to it, ditto the city's fires,
ditto even the river's liquid or Tanimoto's wet sobs
        who clutched it with both hands whether
poling with it or when, in water too deep for it,
        paddling with it. It *could* hear,
& it *did* have, as we've known, eyes with which
        to witness, but it was almost, still, insensate,
& for this it was glad. Blood tried to seep into it,
        at one point a slough of pus & skin slid onto it,
its tip once ground into mouse droppings under Tanimoto's perch,
        but all these reminders washed from it as now
our August moon begins to glow full with viscous color.

The Fish

Empathetic, the fish transformed itself,
        became a burn in the water, encaustic,
turned ochre, then blue, then yellow,
        then red, then swelled like a tickled blowfish,
then burst: that part of itself smelly pus
        plumed into the river, but the rest
kept swimming. By now, it was night. By now,
        what had it learned ex-
cept that the refracted ones above it, the floaters,
        kept calling to it, both the living & the dead,
to intercede, but how, & to what, or whom?
        To the moon? This was no use. It became time
to reconstitute itself. In fact, it became Time,
        our fish in the river, the blunt one,
now strong, now full-bodied again.

The Fish

Our fish, too, had its own relationship with God,
      that day & since, though that day & since are the same.
But its inquiries had less to do with suffering
      than with how it came to possess gold fins
& a tail by which it could propel itself through rivers
      so gracefully, if it didn't say so itself. The phenomenon
of ferryman & boat intrigued, of course,
      but this was nothing personal. The fish did witness,
as we've seen. It was, to be sure, curious, but *why*,
      it wondered aloud to that cloud, did God sometimes
so darken sky that bright gold became only a glint
      in the flowing of the water. & did God want it
to be doing elsewise than just swimming between shores
      or sleeping at night in God's riverbank den?
Sometimes scales on its blunt head flaked from such questions.

The Pole

When, whenever, Tanimoto abandoned the bamboo pole,
      it almost managed to root itself, but couldn't,
no matter how many of its eyes sought a propitious bed.
      But it never lost its gift or propensity for refraction,
line after line reflected & broken, shadowed & broken.
      If we could trace its yellowish movement in water,
we'd see formations of letters as though river were
      its Ouija board, wouldn't we not never?
The pole refracts the word of God, to be sure, even if
      God isn't or, in the end, leaves no one alive
to read. The pole's utilitarian value came to an end—
      though to this day it senses Tanimoto's hands & retains
his fingerprints. Now, in this medium,
      refractedly,
the best it can do is to rot toward beauty.

The Boat

There it is, the *Enola Gay* on display in the American capital,
      drawing visitors into reflection below it.
Now, here, let us raise toward a skylight, too,
      Tanimoto's boat that once received the flash
from this bomber's bomb & in its wood remembers every
      mutation in every organic cell.
It ain't much to look at, no gleaming surfaces, no
      geomentrical certitude, no glass, no
electronics, no name of no mother painted on its bow,
      but we've at least one secret to keep from powers-that-be,
don't we? It's your turn this evening, just before closing,
      when guards aren't looking, to toss
a few peanuts up into Tanimoto's vessel.
      It could be years before we & that last passenger
are found out. It could be decades, or trilliseconds.

Mrs. Aoyama & Me

She was up & about early that morning. Language
      streamed through her mind as it does through
all our minds: phrases & sentences, discon-
      nections & lucidities, splotches of consciousness,
musical syllabics she paid no special attention to ex-
      cept when she did, which was only sporadically
as for all of us . . . . She dressed. She sipped tea. She performed
      whatever familiar rituals, & went outside.
August 6 might or might not have been any particular day for her
      for any particular reason—a birthday, a death.
There might or might not have been a sense of foreboding in her
      because of the war. She did not know that this day
would eventually create a central character in a suite of poetry
      by a boy then only four years old but learning adverbs
instantaneously, timelessly, in the homeland of her enemy.

Song

Now to commence arming America's mega-weapon,
        change the bomb's plugs, whatever they were,
whatever they exactly were, the plugs with their *guh* sound
        occluded in the throat, plugs, *guh*, ugly ironic im-
ploded sound compared to the vowels of *Tanimoto*,
        Aoyama. But God didn't say *Let there be sounds*,
he declared light like the flash through which
        the *Enola Gay* sailed after it released
Little Boy, & our child accomplished its design,
        didn't it? It did. Now we don't know which sounds
might help us sail home from one century to another,
        & another. What's *your* name? I do, *guh*,
get the feeling that you're with me, or will be, won't we?
        It's hard to know just what you & I are asking ex-
cept whether we need to stop singing while we sing.

The Fall

Just before beginning to unwrite this sentence I was thinking
        Just Before might be the title of a collection
of what rememberers remembered doing
        just before. Such books no doubt already exist,
their subject being, whatever their particulars, the chasm between
        human beings' present lives & lives they lived
just before the cataclysm as being the difference between
        being alive in life & dead in it,
for the flash is the fracture point of *tremendum*,
        of refraction itself, brain stem & spinal column
unfused with otherness, just after. We change the plugs. We can't un-
        diagram it, the illness is ir-
reversible, Little Boy falls from the bay, these are seconds
        just before the horrific split of exiles from hope
until their lives are undead even while not even lived.

Letter to Kyoshi Tanimoto

Sir, Mr. Mnemonic, I don't know why I've heretofore
        not mentioned that you were a Methodist pastor ex-
cept no never what isn't does matter doesn't it not ex-
        cept what you experienced while what you did
ministers without diplomas or certification, amen.
        You are a sound in us, not a position. Your congregation
abides both there with you & with the not-yet-born, nor
        does your black hair still not host glints of red
from the firestorm as dragonflies in their iridescence
        seem in their miniature metallic ways to be B-29s or
Japanese suns, but no matter. Beyond us, beyond
        especially me in my melodic gibberishness, you
are the one intelligible one as you transport strangers to another shore.
        My listeners & I will some day be ready. Wait, don't
leave without us, surely you'll not abandon us here.

Letter to Mrs. Aoyama

Ma'am, I was walking my village this afternoon, thinking
        about you. Once in a while I'd stop—as I did
in front of a church, then a clothing store, then
        an antique shop—to check in case I heard a plane
droning overhead, but didn't. From moment to moment I wondered
        if I'd been translated or transliterated or re-
fracted into whatever dimension you suddenly did
        or did not inhabit . . . but I hadn't been. Traffic continued, hex-
agonal stop signs kept stopping cars, pots of marigolds blossomed,
        a school bus yellowed by, my shoes kept containing my feet,
& I knew nothing, I knew, about what had happened to you ex-
        cept that you vanished without pain into
the atomic beyond. My writing to you is just convention,
        of course, you are so far gone. My writing to you
is a mode of thinking, I was thinking, as I was walking,

half in daydream & half in a cloudy empiricism
    that told me my Brockport streets
& the Erie Canal that cuts refractedly through them ex-
    ist in a continuum of time that continues me,
unlike what was your experience, wasn't it not? I mean—
    I mean I meant to mean. I mean
that just before you vanished, we shared an axiomatic reality
    of place & family, of bodies of water, but then
you were suddenly elsewise in your dispersion, or,
    as some would have it, less even than that.
If possible, I'd like for you to sense how my own dis-
    pensations of reason & romance do in-
crease, yes, but not without a resonance of care for you who
    continued along as I do now. But tell me, is your soul
at home, or in a vacuum less than zero?

Time

Some illuminates say that in one way or another
    they've transcended time—maybe hitch-hiking, or drugs,
or long abstinence from sleep, or sex, or the mind's eye
    peering into the annals of lilac, or in dream,
or by way of mnemonic mantra, or, or. There was one moment
    when Mr. Tanimoto's soul concentrated into
everything he'd experienced of cherry trees—seeing touching
    dreaming smelling tasting—until,
at the moment of his momentary transcendence, a blossom
    in its simultaneous myriad colors enveloped him
even while he poled his boat across the river, even while
    traumatized passengers moaned & cried.
What's not never isn't it to understand about this?
    If only we could keep him there, if only, if only . . .
but here that blossom falls, & time resumes our linear agony.

Questions

Couldn't it ever not even be
that as Mrs. Aoyama became less than a non-entity
she or what she had not even not never been
became part of a reverse realm in which even her kimono—
have I mentioned that its gold silk
shadowed its blue?—could never or *did* she in fact retroact
to the point at least of a memory which,
in fact, is more than most such non-entities might even
aspire to? We might consider her in her infinite
divisibilities as, if not somewhere, then still re-
trievable in some loving way for those who loved her.
Couldn't it even not even not be yes that thought itself
taking place in the currents of—couldn't it not?—
God's mind, envelops her as it couldn't if she'd indeed yes not
ceased in all possibilities at least still to be?

The Fish

I read that goldfish have a memory that resets
every thirty seconds or so—this means
they'll overeat & can blow up. But our fish,
the blunt-headed one staying near Tanimoto's boat,
is not a goldfish. It remembers, its heavy head
stores what it sees, & it knows when
it's had enough, as it has at this day's end.
It finds its riverbank den. It uses
its gold fins & its tail to ease its way in,
it rests in silt & gravel, only its gills moving.
It would close its eyes if it could, but it can't,
can't it? Nevertheless, its mind becomes
only the color of the dun water, though synapses
of fire do filter into this medium even down here
in this primordial cave within the burning city.

The Fish

No one has worked at the Hiroshima aquarium long enough
       to know how this particular fish became
part of its collection, nor is this one seen very often
       by those in wetsuits who feed the groupers & sharks
blobs of vitamin-enriched meat, nor does anyone know for sure
       how old this gold-finned one is that has become
something of a rumor or legend for schoolchildren who,
       even if they haven't seen it, do draw it, paint it,
attempt origami enfoldings of it, dream its bulbous forehead
       as a shape sometimes foreboding,
sometimes comforting, write poetry & stories of its origin
       in the sea &, before that, the stars.
For its part, the fish now observes such human activities,
       but all day stays in its cave neither enjoying nor not
the show that persists past the water, past the glass.

River

I'd say chances are good this afternoon that Mr. Tanimoto
       will see the fish that accompanies him—
clarity will reveal the gold-finned one even though
       he or she or it swims in sifting ash
in the shadow of the ferryman's boat. At the same time,
       I'd say that chances improve, too, that Mr. Tanimoto
won't pay close attention, or, if he does, won't know how
       to interpret the blunt-headed one's behavior.
In any case, this is never not something about either of them,
       of course, but about us as we consider
such a scenario—Mr. Tanimoto & this fish—even while
       a whole city's inhabitants define acute pain, stricken
with shock &/or terror, or are already dead. Our minds
       refract by way of our chosen medium, our theme, this river
allowing us to keep our bearing toward the hoped-for shore.

Night Watchman

Word has it that at night the fish lifts out
       of its rock cave in the aquarium
& drones through dim light past sleepers,
       sometimes reversing its orbit, sometimes its level,
sometimes in fact its whole axis until it seems
       to the lone security guard to be not inhabitant
of this city attraction but apparation, just ghostly glints
       of gold: there & now he sees it, there & now he doesn't.
But what's it to him whether or not he's experiencing
       a fish or some illusive attribute of waterlights,
except that his kids are always asking him, "Father,
       did you see it last night, did you see it?"
& except that his wife, too, often asks him whether
       that planet in the water ever answered its own koans.
Let's just leave him there, peering into his dream.

Heat

His batting instructor told the great Sadaharu Oh
       to see with the eye in his hip.
In other words, slugger, get your whole body to perceive
       the seams of whatever hurled heat may be
blazing toward home plate.
       In other words, masters can pluck Zeno's arrows from the air
& redirect bullets with sword blades. On an earthly plane,
       yes, we can see with our knees as we kneel,
with our tongue as we speak 15-line poems made loosely
       of strophes that find the left margin of song & then
indent themselves until closure with the longer line.
       But how could this apply to Mr. Tanimoto?—
no matter how he used his body's countless eyes,
       he could not stop victims' skins from sloughing to the ground,
eyeless. Nor could Mrs. Aoyama raise her average above zero.

Sound

Let's make believe Mrs. Aoyama had not been at Point Zero,
        that she made her way to Mr. Tanimoto's boat,
& boarded. She sits on musty rumpled canvas, the ferryman
        thrusts his bamboo pole into the water, she notices
refraction, the pole entering river from one medium
        & then breaking into another, but no matter,
for the pole's physics hold it together as a force
        for propulsion. Mrs. Aoyama sees a shore
where trees punctuate smoke that drifts, settles,
        lifts, darkens, swirls, lightens, dis-
sipates, forms again. She seems to exist just before,
        leaving flames behind her, except for gold candles
gusting how far down in the water?
        But it's impossible for her to be distracted until
she hears a telltale squeak beneath her.

The Bee

That morning, at first light, Mr. Tanimoto visited a pond
        beside a temple, graygreen reeds
a stone's throw away, & what might have been a crane
        standing still as though dawn had not yet
awakened it. He heard a rasp in the air, a bee
        slowed a few feet from his face, then
sped toward that sheen of water. He wondered if he himself might
        inhabit such a mind, if it might be said
that insects possess mind. In any case,
        he wished an artist were here to paint beauty pure,
even its sound. If only brain were osmotic & could fill
        with essence of pond, temple, morning, Mr. Tanimoto prayed.
As for us, it should be possible, shouldn't it not,
        to allow him time with his thoughts? For once, . . . let's.
Our bee returns to him, buzzes words into his ear.

Thought

I like to think that the bamboo pole was thinking to itself
        that it was glad it was being used like this
instead of being crafted into kitchen utensils, or into
        a piece of furniture, or a doormat, or reduced to slivers
to be driven under someone's fingernails to elicit confession.
        Yes, if it had to be severed from where it grew,
why shouldn't it serve toward transport for Tanimoto,
        that intrepid soul, on that day when it could hear
agony, could see scenes as though etched for Dante's *Inferno*?
        I like to think that the bamboo pole enjoyed tasting
river bottom, & liked seeing how close Tanimoto might thrust it
        toward the self-important fish. Oh how it would like
at least to scratch a few scales from that assured blunt head,
        but why should bamboo think in this pathetic way,
our stout pole of practical use on this of all our days?

Companions

To what extent is it, or is it not, let's say, valid,
        to say that Mrs. Aoyama & the fish are of the same essence?
After all, the latter appears here & there like the nothingness
        into which that woman in her blue kimono was translated;
after all, she had glints of gold sunlight on her cheeks & sleeves
        before that trillisecond of disappearance. Resemblances
abound, her lungs being gills, its movement through water
        being much like hers through air, & what we call the life-
spark sparked/sparks in both. We pose this question
        because something in us tells us they much enjoy
one another's company, & will. Both of them are nowhere,
        aren't they not, & everywhere we sound? The river flows,
time refracts, she is with the fish in their several dimensions,
        no need for us to think our way too deeply into this,
that fish swimming beneath cobblestones, that woman walking in water.

Cosmos

If it is true that only one character inhabits a dream,
> the self, & if it is true that I have fallen

in & out of dream here in this suite of never not mind Hiroshima,
> part of me might unify Aoyama, Tanimoto,

the boat, the bamboo pole, the blunt-headed & gold-finned fish;
> but if it is not true that all dreamed persons & objects

are in fact dreams of self, then I read myself as being
> the creature under canvas that you'd forgotten, admit it,

until I just now mentioned it again. But when I think
> of what I've said about it, I see where I did place myself

on that day when, in my metaphysics of bafflement & story,
> I hid within history, my hallucinogen.

If it is true that a rodent nests under canvas during Tanimoto's crossings,
> then maybe this squeaking entity posits either

myself thinking about dreaming, or dreaming, or neither.

Stasis

Who is the mother huddled in Tanimoto's boat,
> a shawl over her child, a dragonfly umbrella

blocking both from our sight?
> She might be the one we've been looking for,

but we can't quite see her. She is bent over her child
> in an attitude that reminds us of so many paintings,

black madonnas, she whose name is Worldsorrow,
> whose child may or may not be breathing.

How is it that our history has come to this,
> we wonder, as Tanimoto's pole thrusts

refraction after refraction into the river?
> She has never not been here on this boat

that moves & does not move as the current
> moves & does not move as the child moves

and does not move as we move & do not move.

The Fish

A heavy-headed fish swims through history
      in the depths of the *Konzentrationslager*
& the Balkans & under African dirt at Darfur beneath
      Nanjing & Wounded Knee & Troy & Masada
its gills keep sifting as it swims the ditch at My Lai
      nor does it not never persist swimming among
roots of trees where slaves were tortured & hanged
      & there it is at Babi Yar & there in Europe again
beneath the ancient Roman Colloseum it seems
      empowered to be everywhere at once a swimming
stasis within continuum even beneath Jerusalem.
      But, every night, it finds its cave in Hiroshima.
It rests there. It does not consolidate wisdom or doctrine
      about where in hell on earth it has been. It rests.
It hears *That Which Does Not Speak*. It swims forth again.

A Presence

One night long before that human August day,
      the fish felt something stirring within itself,
thus ventured from its cave into the slow moonlit current.
      Back then, its forehead was rounded,
& its whole being, not just its fins, flashed with gold.
      What a sight it would have been,
but no people existed to see it, no dictionaries, there was
      no city, but it itself did not think about this.
It swam out. It swam into the lunar water. It did
      not have a destination, nor did it foresee
a future when gold would diminish from its torso,
      its head assume mal-aesthetic proportions.
This night, it did not worry whether or not it would
      or would not ever find its way back to its cave.
This night, moonlight swims with it, candles it,

doesn't it not? But now time is itself in us
        & with us again, for here is the shadow
of Tanimoto's boat, the one he borrowed
        from the dead. The fish does not wonder where
it itself has been, or for how long—its mind
        refracts, a bamboo pole has eyes
& almost impales it, the fish adjusts its position
        beneath the ferryman's boat,
but hears human weeping about which it, even
        if it would, can do nothing. How long has all this
wordlessness been going on, & what light was that
        that stunned even microdust the fish sifted
through its gills? But no use our trying to deploy
        language to try to gain some access to how
a fish apprehends time or moonlit &/or bomb-lit water,

isn't there not ever not? But we do, but the fish
        grows tired of all this, & we'll not,
from this point backward, follow it again unless
        in the scheme of things God restores its gold.
Meanwhile, onomatopoetical, from under canvas,
        our little bewhiskered pal squeaks as it breathes
the scent of Mr. Tanimoto's sweat, & of blood,
        & of compromised skin, & of Mrs. Aoyama's dispersed aura.
Now, even the flowing water is an embalming fluid
        if not never when we can ever lift them from it,
if you know what I mean to mean. We evolve,
        we visit the *Enola Gay* in its museum, we sense
in lights that swim in the air around it a presence,
        fish-shaped, redemptive no not nor angelic,
but, yes, auratic, suffused with our time in Time.

The Decision

One day, in the hands of a corporation, the bamboo pole
  thrust through ocean floor into a cavern of oil,
& the oil exploded upward through & past the pole,
  thousands & hundreds of thousands of gallons,
tens of thousands & millions & hundreds of millions of barrels,
  such volumes of crude that all the world's coasts
blackened with carcinogens, wildlife perished, human beings
  retreated inland to the last shade, strangled one another,
& choked out. Then, after timeless eons, bacteria began
  to begin again, primordial forests rose, the oil subsided,
the earth became pristine, God wondered whether Eden
  might be worth another try, decided, didn't God not,
no, but then, didn't He &/or She &/or It reconsider, or not . . . .
  A fish appeared, all gold among riverbank roots, but now
who do we see but that courageous ferryman, Mr. Tanimoto!

Watercolor

Other characters here would be deflection—never mind
  that snail, that crab, that stately crane
spearing newts & frogs at first light when river
  seems to emanate from between the temples
of God, who evolves. But the whorl of that shell, & the snail's
  tendril antennae. The crab's ocher-green claws,
its eyes on tensile stalks. The crane's sharp beak
  this August morning glinting shadowed silver & gold—
snail, crab, crane in, yes, this evolving painting
  as the grayblue river delivers itself beyond them forever,
but stays. When is there ever too much beauty
  for us to consider if not now in the time before?
But now all three hear what approaches from the air,
  they & countless others of their kind can't know what is about
to refract our planet's every eye & ear, every cell of color.

Our Nest

Let's hide under the canvas. We'll still at first hear
　　　　cries & moans, & smell burnt skin, burnt hair,
but won't know the origins of so much suffering. A Zen master
　　　　learned to ignore the loud ticking of an alarm clock
close to him, & hear instead a wrist watch six feet distant.
　　　　In the same Tao, here under canvas, we'll hear,
after a long time, after as long as we require, only
　　　　waterplash while our boat reaches the far shore.
Water beneath us, water to the sides of us, water
　　　　in front of us & behind us. What was it
we were thinking of not thinking about? Let's hope for sleep
　　　　here where water laves us with its narcotic plashing.
I'm not sure about you, but I don't ever not never, do I,
　　　　intend to abandon this nest, or could I, even if,
in the end, Tanimoto pulls our boat from the river.

Time Hearts

A long time went by .... So much time went by,
　　　　that Time itself realized itself passing,
if we can believe. Time sensed itself as being
　　　　no longer timeless, as the Ota rivers kept wearing
away their banks, & even our moon seemed worn out
　　　　from being rubbed by eons of sensate water,
if we can believe. But if we can't believe—
　　　　as Tanimoto & Aoyama can't quite believe—
we'll enter the mind of the blunt-headed one,
　　　　to feel how time does gill by
within Time. The bomb recedes into flakes & genes
　　　　just as the fish swims away from us,
just as memorial sites despite their mirrors
　　　　(& reflecting pools) & stopped clocks ...
evoke the dead from our dead historical hearts.

Subject Matter

I've got to say goodbye now, friends,
    companions to this reverie of mine—
something else has been occurring, an upwelling,
    a degradation of immense proportions so that you,
Mr. Tanimoto & Mrs. Aoyama, cannot be with me
    suddenly to disappear or to ferry the stricken
toward green; so that you, bamboo pole, cannot see
    with multitudinous eyes; nor you, fish, avoid
the pus plume; nor you, bewhiskered one under canvas,
    sniff vegetation on that far shore. Hiroshima
recedes, the face of our moon in its river clogs with crude,
    that romantic head loses its reflective power,
goes gelid in radioactive water.
    As a poet predicted, "Universal darkness buries all."
My poembooms deteriorate in tides of atomic oil.

The Forest

In my dream I saw Tanimoto pull his boat
    into a gas station, tether it
to a pump. I don't know if that was Mrs. Aoyama with him,
    but someone else, too, was behind
a windshield mounted on his bow. I thought it strange
    not that he or they were there, but that I was—
after all, I hadn't yet earned that dimension within which
    such refraction, such translation might occur.
The nozzle reached like an umbilical cord into his side,
    it might have been bamboo. I thought it took
eons for him to fill up, I could smell fumes
    from the ancient forest distilled—then,
as though nothing extraordinary were happening, he angled
    our boat back into the river of traffic,
turned to wave us all goodbye, & submerged.

Gold

Beloveds, it is not as though you are family, or even
        close friends whose hands I have shaken
or with whom I have broken bread or knelt in prayer,
        or *ohmmm*. It is rather that I love you for using you,
for how . . . malleable you are, if the truth be told—
        Tanimoto, Aoyama, bamboo, fish: gold
I can hammer out in sheets or spin into tackle.
        Beloveds, it is not, then, that I won't miss you,
but you are not . . . rooted . . . in me, & this turns out
        best for both of us or else
you wouldn't not never have ever not come to be,
        at least here, forever. The cities darken, the world
screeches to alleycat cries & then is heard nor seen no more
        by human ears & eyes, but you, yes, like gold,
remain, & cannot tarnish through even eons undersea.

Sayonara

Long ago, on Long Island, when I was a boy, I'd bike
        to ponds a couple-three miles away & to a lake
with an Algonquin name, Ronkonkoma, which might have meant
        bottomless. One late-winter morning after first thaw
I found several coins in the ice-washed sands, & a sodden
        five-dollar greenback among waterweeds.
One mid-summer evening when I needed to be home,
        I stood instead to watch sunset burn that water,
then fall behind pavilions & a treeline on the far shore.
        There were bats then, & birdcalls, & the green smells
of my mostly uphill ride home past Spectacle Pond,
        & crickets, & the *whoosh* of my tires on tar.
That sunset stayed/stays in my mind, the bursts
        of neural fire, the crimson beauty, the feeling that nothing
could possibly extinguish that sun, & then didn't.

The Candle: New Poems

Und Zeit geht hin,und Zeit nimmt zu, und Zeit
ist vie ein Rückfall einer langen Krankheit.

(& Time passes, & Time adds to itself, & Time
is like a falling back into abiding sickness.)

Rainer Maria Rilke
("Requiem for a Friend")

October: grapes hung like the fists of a girl
gassed in her prayer. *Memory,*
I whisper, *stay awake.*

Ilya Kaminsky
"A Toast"

Butterfly

Terezin girl with pencil, she draws.
Draftsmen of crematoria, they draw.
SS, a luger in his holster, he draws.
Diarist's diary, it draws.
Jewess at the Commandant's bath, she draws.

Selector, he draws. The trains, they draw.
The dead & soon-dead, they draw.
Smoke from a chimney, it draws.
Shoah curtains, they draw. O butterfly,
draw me, draw near to me, draw from me.

1939: The Medal

My mother's father met Adolf Hitler
on a Bremerhaven pier.
The Fuhrer, fellow veteran,
pressed his cheek against

his comrade's temple who'd escaped
from the Russians in 1917.
Each time my mother told this story,
my grandfather saw tears

in the great man's blue eyes,
the Fuhrer's embrace grew longer,
his respect for August Wörmke deeper,
those blue eyes bluer until,

now, here, this relation is his medal,
pure silver, nothing to corrupt it
but rumors of allusive context.
Her two heroes eclipse that pier.

Blutzeugtag: Blood Oath Day

Today, as *SS*, I rededicate myself to you,
Mein Fuhrer: *I believe in you,*
I will wait for you, I will follow you.

That said, I place my forehead
against *your* serrated blade,
my lyric. Do not be afraid

to carve me &/or slay for me.
I was born for this loyalty
to form & beauty. Be ready:

I believe in you,
I will wait for you,
I will follow you.

Flame

Marching files of *SS* became candles,
guttered in blurred goosesteps,
slowed to stillness in hardening wax,
heads lit with flame that swept
from under helmets. Next,
a mass grave, the *SS* candles extinguished.

When I was a boy, farmer Hans Wenzel
taught me how to candle eggs,
revolve them slowly over an oval hole
in a box he'd contrived wherein
a lightbulb burned. I peered
into translucence for veins, blood-

spots, shadows of beginning bones,
spectral tracery of angels' feathers—
eggs Mrs. Wenzel wouldn't boil
or bake into cakes. Decades later, I dream
those immortal *SS*, yes, but am unable
to candle their essence of evil . . . .

How indomitable they were, the Nazis
whose divisions thundered across Europe,
who administered the death camps until
they & their creations never ceased to be,
their candles burning to go dead in history,
amen, until the next time they candle me.

Testimony of Christa Schröder

I was the Fuhrer's senior secretary. You ask me
of his directives concerning eastern *Untermenschen*.
I will tell you this: one spring day in 1941,
Heinrich Himmler left our office after two hours
alone with our leader. He sat down in the chair

beside my desk, buried his head in his hands,
said, *"Mein Gott, mein Gott*, what am I expected to do?"
Much later, when I heard what had been done,
I assumed that that was the very day the Fuhrer
ordered Herr Himmler to exterminate the Jews.

The Murderer

Mauthausen, an *SS* bragged to a Frau Strasser:
"Today I killed another two inmates."
"How did you do that?" the office worker asked.
"I chased both of them into a vat of liquid manure,
threw a crate over them, and stood on top of it
until they drowned." . . . Now, here, his own head

protrudes from that manure. Yes,
I can see it. Now I want to step on it.
Yes, I have stepped on it, he is choking.
S, I say, *S*, you *SS* Aryan bastard,
& heel my weight on this sadist's *Kopf*
until he disappears.

Interrogation

A report to Himmler by one Viktor Brack:
tests completed on mass sterilization by X-ray.
Conclusion: two machines each at twenty installations

could treat three to four thousand subjects a day.
Offices would be established to which *Untermenschen*
would be ordered to answer whatever questions.

During such interrogations, secret irradiation would occur—
men requiring higher intensities for shorter duration
(two minutes), women lower intensities for longer

(three minutes). It would be weeks before these noticed
assorted burns & realized what had happened—
but this awareness, Brack said, would be irrelevant.

Equipment for each office would be about RM 25,000,
plus the cost of the facility itself, & protective shielding
for those who administered these procedures .... *Heil Hitler* ....

Are you still with me? Do you still feel, as I do, history's
background radiation? Can you find it in you to trust me
even while melanomas bubble up in us? Comrade,

shall we not together curse Brack's mind to heaven?
Here is your lead suit. We must shield ourselves
while answering the Third Reich's questions.

Civilization

Imagine yourself in the mind of Goebbels,
my poem. Imagine it is March 27, 1942,
while he writes in his journal

the procedure employed is not to be described,
there won't be much left of the Jews—
60 percent of them will have to be liquidated

keep writing yourself, liquidate your own mind
the punishment the Jews are being subjected to,
though barbaric, is entirely deserved

poem in the mind of Goebbels, accept
the slaughter of families, of whole villages
One can't allow oneself to be ruled by sentimentality

so write yourself, execute yourself like this,
fall into your own grave, & an end to it.

Reminder

A survivor remembered two young Jewish men,
intensely religious, awaiting execution.
Before the Germans shot them,
the two scratched their own faces, scratched out

parts of their beards—this, by their laws,
"is forbidden, to inflict themselves like that."
The witness said that at the end the two
"regretted what they were and what they were made."

This ends there, but does not. This is what
the murderers that day did to these young men,
not what they inflicted on themselves, Heyen,
but what in the end your iniquitous blood did to them.

Sailing to Danzig

Autumn, 1944, Jewish prisoners on a German boat
sailing to Danzig. On deck, one prayed aloud.
Below, candles threw eerie shadows.
Around them, history swelled & pitched.

Once out of nature, I don't want to see or hear anything
except the candles, their susurrus of light,
only their light, not those grotesque shadows,
so I'll press my face close to their wicks, their auras.

Here, for once, I can't sense anything except light.
I'm so close to the Jews I feel heat on my forehead.
I must be careful that my skin does not sear.
Even when I close my eyes, I experience only light.

Who says I can't subvert history by staring into candles?
I've tried other methods, but Jews were murdered
in time forever to belong to the moon, its tides,
& to me. But the candles! How bright they are!

Otto Pressburger, 18, at Birkenau, 1942

We went to work to build roads—Kapos and *SS* men
supervised us. There was one Jew from our town,

tall and strong, from a rich family. The Kapo spotted
gold teeth and said give them to me.

The man answered he could not, but the Kapo again said
give them to me, but the man still said he could

not give up his gold teeth. The Kapo took
a shovel and hit him over the head until

the tall man fell down. The Kapo turned him over
and put the shovel at his throat and stood on it.

He broke the man's neck and used the shovel to get
the teeth out of his mouth. Another Jew asked

how you could do this. The Kapo killed him the same way.
He warned us don't ask questions, mind your own business.

That evening we carried twelve bodies back to barracks.
He killed them just for fun. This happened the first day.

Luger

But is this the story of Paul Lieberman,
one of the camp favorites, even of the Germans,
19 years old, or of Schwetke, *SS* corporal,
who shot him, or of the survivor who was there,
who remembers?: Lieberman stole a loaf of bread
to pass to his sister in another camp.
The *SS* beat him, then took him to the cemetery
where prisoners worked with sledges
to break up stones for paving roads. On the way,
Schwetke, not until then known for his brutality,
shot the young man in the back of his head . . . .

The witness & five others buried Paul there where
they'd worked to pulverize Jewish gravestones.
But does this story with its named perpetrator
now belong to that *SS* corporal, Schwetke,
or to Paul Lieberman, or to the pseudonymous teller
in Henry Greenspan's *On Listening to Holocaust Survivors*?
Or does it now of necessity belong to me, to us,
or does it now belong to the one entity, poetry,
that remembers it while at the same time knowing
it must hear what cannot be said,
what is left out, what no one knows or knew, period.

Determination

"I'll send you there," said the Lagerführer,
pointing to the chimney.

Said the Lagerführer, pointing to the chimney,
"I'll send you there."

Pointing to the chimney, the Lagerführer said,
"I'll send you there."

Said the Lagerführer, "I'll send you there,"
pointing to the chimney.

Pointing to the chimney, "I'll send you there,"
the Lagerführer said.

One way or another—begin reading anywhere—
he'll send you there.

Katyń, 1941: The Germans

"Each morning the Germans went round with guns
finishing off those no longer able to stand up.
The Germans used their rifle butts to smash
the hands of men holding their comrades upright.
The sick fell to the ground, the Germans

"piled them onto carts, stripped them
of their boots and clothing, hauled them to a pit,
unloaded them *with pitchforks* and threw them
into the pit alongside the corpses. A sprinkling
of quicklime, and that was that."

Sport

In late June 1942, *SS* guards,
bored, ravenous for sport,
drove dozens of Jews up
from the Mauthausen pit, 186 steps,

jabbed them with rifle butts
until they plunged over the edge.
These *SS* wits were heard to shout
"Achtung, parachutists!"

Eyes

Interviewing "Lydia," Henry Greenspan noticed
her expression did not change even as she told

of a yard filled with dead babies covered with blood,
"nor was there any perceptible alteration in the tone

"or cadence of her voice." Thus he was surprised
to see that she was crying, her eyes

"shedding tears as though they, too, had a mind
and a memory of their own.". . . We'll remember

how her eyes spoke Kaddish for her,
her each tear miscible with another.

Avraham Tory: Diary from the Kovno Ghetto

"Babies were taken out and placed on the ground
in the stone-paved hospital courtyard,
their tiny faces turned skyward.

"Soldiers of the third squad of the German Police
passed between them. They stopped for a moment.
Some kicked the babies with their boots.

"The babies rolled a little to the side,
but some soon regained their belly-up position,
their faces turned toward the sky."

The diarist turned those faces toward the sky,
but the sky had no eyes in its passive face
as the faceless German Police murdered the babies.

Shekhinah

in a wood.
In my dream she stood in an open area
A machine that looked

through roots
like a huge scorpion cut a ditch
behind her, her aura

snapped into her,
wavered, she became candleflame, a bullet
she fell into the ditch

over her,
& sputtered out. The scorpion pulled earth
at the same time stinging her grave repeatedly . . . .

but I do keep
Mine is usually a sensibility of body & money,
a candle lit beside my easy chair,

that I experience
& do write in my diary of the glimmer of spirit
almost daily. I pray to primal powers

who are many.
that I be worthy of all those who love & need me,
Nor am I resigned

who set atrocity into motion
that a dreamed scorpion or hidden perpetrators
killed beauty forever,

stinging the grave
but that machine out of my psyche kept
of the mother who spoke in tongues,

                    bathed them
who fed the Jews with milk & candleflame,
        in story & balm. As for me,

            or it came to power
I was either born with this scorpion within,
        by way of the holy

            but whatever it is
which itself is terrified by that which came to be, . . .
        that I've just now said,

        a study of the Holocaust diary:
consider David Patterson in *Along the Edge of Annihilation*,
        "Exceeding the horror

            waited until many
"of slaughtering pregnant mothers, it seems that the Nazis
        of these women held their babies

            this being the brutal essence
"in their arms before murdering them and their infants with them," . . .
        of "the ontological nature

            engraved in my dream,
"of the assault on the mothers of Israel" the ones
        that this German machine

            Katzelson cries out,
keeps electrocuting through the sod: verily, diarist Yitzhak
        "This murdrous German nation!

                women
    "That was their chief joy! To destroy
            with child!"

Definition for the New Bible

Kindergarten:
a site
for the Nazis
to gather
Jewish children,

to truck them
away, to mur-
der them, to
harvest them: gar-
den of flowers.

Bayer Co. to the Auschwitz Authorities

"the transport of 150 women
arrived in good condition.
However, we were unable
to obtain conclusive results
because they died during experiments.

"We kindly request
that you send us
another group of women
to the same number
and at the same price."

The Arrival Sonnet: Dagmar Ostermann

"A figure approached us.
She looked like a walking skeleton;
she seemed to consist of eyes only.
She asked us where we came from.
We said, 'From Ravensbrück,'
and then we asked, 'Where are we here?'
She said, 'You are in Auschwitz.'
That was the first time I heard the name."...

      [I've refracted Ostermann's arrival story
      into eight lines, Auschwitz having been /
      being another mode of discourse,
      where we are as we return within
      syntactical irreversibles to words
      come to consist of eyes only.]

Prayer

It could be that after Auschwitz there should be no prayer, that prayer is barbaric, inhumane, divisive, greedy, selfish, egocentric to the point of monomania & imbecility. That is, for me to give thanks to or to beseech my problematic deity for my own *blessings*—is this the most absurd word in our religious vocabularies?—of family & place & health, or for me to ask for healing & secure future & heaven for myself & others of my particular tribe, is an act rife with betrayal of the tortured & slaughtered, the lost who still scream & claw in the gas chambers. Such so-called communion with God is doggedly ridiculous & stupidly irrational. But true poetry (which integrates, which loves), even when it seems to be in control of itself this control may of course seem to embody an obscene non-empathic expression of pre-Holocaust aspirations for beauty & order—but especially when its rhythmical speech becomes silence—true poetry may not be our redemption or salvation but, still, one justification to go on living. & now may this declarative paragraph explode into smoke & voices that dissipate into agonized prayer & ash just out of sight & hearing above the death camps.

Prayer

I dreamed an animal over an *SS* grave—
night, the moon, urine candleflame.

I rose from there in my uniform,
death's head tattoo stigmata in each palm,

enraged to kill anything in my vision—
that animal, you who hear & witness, the moon

glimmering softly on this cemetery as I wake
into sleep again. Rest now, my soul, in black.

Absence

What it is, what it can never be other than,
the survivor recounting a gray morning
when his work Kommando returned to ghetto,
entered where corpses lay everywhere, when,

this gray cadaver of a morning,
"even the Ukrainian guards were scared and confused,"
& not even those returning seemed alive
as they entered the mystical ghetto, even

the guards acting as though dead
where no sound of sound is recorded
out of & into the vacuum of our dead time
out of & into the vacuum of our dead poem.

Night Parable

The dead look down into a well
& see water, yes, but also a candle
whose flame wavers, but, yes, a candle
in that water, candling that black water;
no, candled by that black water.

Sound

It is not as though she had not told her story
many times before, & it is not as though
she herself did not realize how her story
did change each time she told it although

she desired to be faithful to it as she remembered it,
but it was as though sometimes as she told it—
at its center a brute smashed a child against brick—
it receded to where she was before what

had happened did happen, didn't it?
While she stood there on the sidewalk, that soldier
seized the infant by one leg & smashed it, brick
splattering with blood & skull, that baby girl

mute now except for the sound of her head . . .
the sound of her story which, however told,
we of necessity tend not to hear but with which,
must it, mustn't it, it must conclude.

Volcano: Testimony of Albert Hartl

In Kiev during the hot summer of 1942,
Colonel Paul Blobel—according to history
a drunk & a monster—drove Hartl
to a general's dasha: "At one moment—
it was just getting dark—we were passing
a long ravine. I noticed strange movements of earth,
clumps of earth rising into the air as if
by their own propulsion—and there was smoke:
it was like a low-toned volcano, as if
lava burned just below the ground.
Blobel laughed, pointed with his arm
to that ravine at Babi Yar and said,
'Here lie my thirty thousand Jews.'"

Hitler Street

The strip left from hair roughly shaved
down the middle of a prisoner's skull:
SS called this strip *Hitler Strasse*—

they could see their Fuhrer in his black boots
stride from back of the Jews' heads overhill
to their foreheads. He had his dog Blondi with him,

& led a parade, & lifted his arm, *Heil*,
to adoring crowds as the whole Reich
followed him to the crematorium.

Of Covenant

In Vilna Ghetto in 1942 the *SS* allowed the Jews
a library. In his diary,

Yitskok Rudashevski notes the circulation of the 100,000th book,
but does not mention

its title. "The book unites us with the future," he writes, "the book
unites us with the world."

Surely in that 100,000th book were words in Hebrew or Yiddish
for water, wind, fire,

for prayer, pupil, heaven, tree, holy, sin, covenant, angel,
son, daughter, candle,

& thousands more. Surely, the killers knew what most were, but not
their order or the power by which

the soul comes to eventual volume, to aleph, to Israel
in our new bible's skull.

Axe

Vet Jack E., testifying in 1997, said he'd heard
a noise downstairs. He asked his buddy
to cover him. He went below
"and there was a big *SS* trooper down there

"chopping up bodies with an axe, heads and torsos
and everything else all around," for the incinerators.
The *SS* just looked at him, turned around,
went back to work. The man was crazy,

Jack said: "He didn't know what he was doing—
he had no idea." Jack took the axe out of his hands where
in that cellar, despite our soldier's courage,
the perpetrators still dismember us.

Gypsies

Fifty years later a former *SS* doctor says
Mengele changed viewpoints several times,
for example regarding gypsies who all,
as not worthy to live, must be gassed.
Nein, save them, they're so artistically gifted.

Let us create in our minds a gypsy painting—
horses with flowered bridles & saddles
in a forest clearing under a full moon:
you can almost hear violins.
Surely, a beautiful full-skirted young woman

will soon part branches & approach the horses . . .
but I am so sick of this that I can't
stomach myself, or you: the way we concoct
a scene, a painting; the way we imagine
something to render horror melodic, . . .

but I am so glad for this that I can't
not praise myself, or you: the way we choose
to hear violins & see that woman; the way
we change our demented minds toward the better,
desiring to spare the gifted ones.

Exile Diptych

1. Mounds

In various survivors' memoirs, there is a stopping point at night in winter along the forced march. Most of the sick & starving bedraggled ones have to fall on the ground in their rags where they are, while a few lucky ones find a semblance of shelter in a barn or behind the slats of a chicken coop through which crystalline snowflakes drift & eventually cover the sleepers. Their captors drink turnip or corn spirits commandeered from local farmers, slumber in thick coats, keeping their rifles warm. Now & then, they roast a chicken or a few potatoes in the coals. At first light, these guards will shout & kick the mounds of snow, & the march to who knows where will resume.

But some of these mounds will not respond to the boots or rifle butts. These bodies under the blanket of white will remain here where they could not be further from anywhere. They could not be further from here, or from anywhere, if they were on another star. These mounds have assumed, now, their full station of exile: they nor we know who they are; they nor we will ever be able to visit them there in history where they remain, not even if we sought out their roads or made memorials of those coops & barns.

Nevertheless, let us meet at the Tomb of the Exile. But not to remember them—an impossibility. Let us, on an appointed night every winter, meet at the windblown Tomb to realize that we cannot even light the candles we've brought forth from our hearts. No, it is no use, the wicks do not catch, the beeswax remains frozen, aura is only a fable from the fairy tales. We hereby renew a necessary knowledge. Here at this place we cannot ignite candles. The only action left for us now is to return to our homes where & when we can.

2. The Candle

A friend forwarded him the link to a declaration of mission from Yad Vashem. Yes, the survivors, the witnesses, those who could swear that they were there, that their very eyes had seen what hundreds of books of testimonies & hundreds of researched histories averred, were almost all gone, would soon all be gone. Therefore, a covenant of remembrance with the future remained necessary, crucial, said the declaration.

Not a word of the passionate Yad Vashem statement was not true, was not spoken from fierce faith & resolve, but nothing in it was new to him. He did not know how he could continue to stay awake within that past when even innocent children were . . . when the gas . . . when the flesh pyres . . .

Still there remained for him the balm of his own books. Some of his poems, those that seemed to come from rhythmic wild places within him that were not of him, those that seemed to resist his soundings of them, were new for him each time he read them. He did not know if he had in him the writing of even one more of them—he seemed at 70 to be exiled now from those places wherein he'd spoken them—but he'd written plenty enough of them, or, somehow, had heard & recorded them. He wondered what the writers of the Yad Vashem declaration might make of them, but was willing to go to his grave not knowing. He did not want to be judged. Maybe, it occurred to him, he wanted to be sung.

But he could not face this possibility, did not want to think about it. It was as though his poems were themselves perpetrators, that even as they remembered & grieved, they were themselves ravenous for praise & remembrance. But even as he sometimes considered this dimension of his work—are lyrics work?—he could not condemn himself, & for this he condemned himself. No, he did not. The ultimate exile, damning & proper. Literary. But it comforted him, still, that his poems now existed & belonged in largest part to themselves. Exile within exile.

Nihilism Crematorium

Every poem has to answer the question "So what?"
Otherwise, it's just an open mouth.
Sadist Striegel at Mauthausen, e.g.,
ordered prisoner Lewkowitz to open his mouth wide
to receive bread, but, instead, Striegel threw

stones & chips of coal into his Jew's maw.
Nor could Lewkowitz close his eyes or he'd be beaten.
"So what?" Our answers have to do with bread,
coal, open eyes, fear, humiliation, a sadist's sport,
but "So what?" With poetry. But "So what?"

Sonnet Ending in Trite Rhyme

After not seeing Hitler for weeks, Albert Speer
looked at that face & thought, *"Mein Gott,*
how could I not have seen how ugly he is:
this broad nose, this sallow skin? Who is this man?"

Fuhrer enters our room & moves quickly to Speer,
holding out his hand. As never before, Speer feels
bone-deep fatigue—it's the unfamiliar ugliness
of one he had adored as no other, ever.

In *Paradise Lost* Satan becomes uglier & uglier
as Hitler did for his architect & armaments minister.
Enough. That broad nose & sallow skin, & more—
even the ugly one's boots clicking on history's floor

as he moves to Speer, his hand held like breath.
The Reich's ugliness fatigues us to the point of death.

Beauty

1.
I fashioned an *SS* officer
from titanium & leather,
welded a purest silver
death's head to his breast.

He stood my height in black boots,
& as for his eyes, I didn't want blue—
I wanted amber fused with ruby
so that candlelight from his head

when it exited might seem
transluminous with blood.
Midnights, to sound our inner sanctums,
I injected him with lightning,

turned him, set him marching
into history among his victims—
his starved, his maimed, his tortured,
his millions of Jews gassed & cremated,

& what became of him became of me
& what became of me becomes of you
& what becomes of you becomes of me
in twenty lines of aberrant beauty.

2.
I fashioned an *SS* doll to resemble
Irma Grese of Auschwitz—
blonde, slim, symmetrically beautiful
with rose-petal lips.

To make my fetish a sadist
I defaulted her brain's microchip
to history's lurid obscene,
Mein Kampf & *The Elders of Zion*

& Eichmann's punctual trains
& the secret speeches of Himmler
who praises such work for the Fuhrer
as must never on earth be written.

Midnights, I watch her whip
ears from Jewish heads,
pummel necks & spines,
polish her boots with blood,

& what became of her became of me
& what became of me becomes of you
& what becomes of you becomes of me
in forty lines of aberrant beauty.

The Maggots Speak

After he crafted that *SS* officer
from titanium & leather,
& conceived for both of them a helpmate,
sadist Irma Grese,

after he bulldozed
a mass grave
into a glass box the size of a freightcar,
he fell for the last time in love

with his own creation,
with how his poems intoned
the sound of something said
that couldn't be disinterred:

his sentences slashed toward art
that might rhythm into dream
that might redeem the murdered
in cerements of form,

into history's grotesqueries of whom
he himself was one
whose epitaph might read . . .
but never mind.

When such as we take wing
we carry victims' ashes
to pollinate dead fields
into memory & madness.

We'll candle each Shoah tongue
& chorus here all night
for those condemned by song
whose subject sickens light.

Poem

~~Germans, Germans,~~
Imokh Shemam
(may their names be eradicated)
~~God damn them~~

~~may they decompose in blood~~
~~clotted uniforms~~
~~Germans, Germans,~~
Imokh Shemam

~~God damn the Germans~~
~~cursed among men~~
~~may they meet Golem~~
Imokh Shemam

~~may golem tear them~~
~~limb from limb~~
~~these civilized Germans~~
Imokh Shemam

~~demonic Germans~~
~~to hell with them~~
~~to the crematorium~~
Imokh Shemam

The Candle

My votive had burned down through its middle,
left a fretwork to one side of its flame.
I could bend this warm wax inward,
& did, & it, too, was consumed.

I'd been reading a survivor's words translated
from the German. She'd managed, at Auschwitz,
when she'd heard her father's transport had arrived,
to smuggle food to him before he was gassed.

My candle kept burning, as it would
for a couple more hours. At one point I pushed
another barracks of honey-amber toward the flame,
& this, too, melted & drew upward into the wick . . . .

That survivor survived. She said she did not
feel vengeful, but I who was not there,
who did not suffer, lust to resurrect those maniacs
to kill them. And you, my listener, don't speak

of forgiving the Devil, not while I'm
writing by candlelight in the scheme
of candled time. May the survivor,
who has since died, candle us, her testimony

a flame of dread that keeps readers
companionable company. Let this votive
burn down to night.
Let us inhale curls of translated smoke.

Kurt M. Regarding the Shofar

This was October, 1944, at Terezin.
Cantor Levy from Berlin started to blow the shofar tone.
As he blew, he found the most beautiful long-held tone.
It was so beautiful until it seemed ... off-key ....

At that moment, at the height of our expectations,
at the height of hope that our prayers could be answered,
the train whistle started. We were stunned.
It was the train whistle that ruined the shofar's tone.

Voller Zug

Full train arriving at Treblinka in 4 to 11 hours
depending on origin; then departure of the *leere Zug*,
4½ to 10 hours later, absent the ones made
short work of: e.g., 40,000 Jews from Bialystok,
Feb. 9 to Feb. 13, 1945—five trains, *volle Züge*
arriving each day at 12:10 p.m., empties

leaving at exactly 9:18, absent all those
murdered in our fortunate absence, clackety-
clack on steel along our receding lines,
all those children there, & gone, families
of *volles Herz*, unless memory never empties,
& even then. Unless, full heart. But even then.

Dandelions: The Survivor

Ellen Stine spent WWII underground in Berlin.
Her first liberator was a Russian
who had fought all the way from Moscow

dragging a WWI machine gun on a rope.
He made her to understand he wanted coffee.
Afraid, she motioned him into her rubble shelter

& boiled what she had: muddy ersatz,
lump of sugar, thimble of goat's milk.
He ordered her to test it. She did, then

he closed his eyes to sip the sweetened sawdust
& ambrosial muck . . . . Well, it was spring.
He did not rape her. Soon, across Europe,

dandelions simmered in frying pans. Still,
now, that soldier hauls his weapon through destruction
in Ellen's mind, helping to ease us here.

Meditation

Rabbi Moshe Weiss visited Bedzin in Poland
where 25,000 Jews had lived before the war.
Now, only one Jew remained, a Mr. Schwartz.

Rabbi Weiss says nothing else about this Mr. Schwartz,
not even whether or not they met. We'll picture Schwartz,
however, walking under autumn oaks, squirrels

skittering over leaves in search of acorns.
Nor are Mr. Schwartz's thoughts large & melodious
as those of Walt Whitman when he walked beneath trees,

or of his master, Emerson, who wrote "the soul is light."
Our Mr. Schwartz's thoughts remain epitome
of the still-suffusing vapors of *Zyklon-B*.

Insanity

Supposedly, this happened: a mother killed & roasted her baby
        so that she,

by rubbing its fat into her husband's body, could soothe
        his rheumatism.

Supposedly, this happened in Germany in the seventeenth century.
        It could be

she loved him that fiercely, & there might be more babies, but just
        one husband.

Such a marriage of patriotism & ingenuity: Bergen-Belsen, Buchenwald,
        Dachau, Gross-

Rosen, Ravensbrück, Treblinka, e.g., &, of course, not last & not least,
        Auschwitz.

Angel

I see a German housewife rubbing fat
onto her rheumatic husband's skin.
Oh how he has suffered, & this balm
cannot hurt. She must do whatever she can.

We don't know if she has told him,
or if he begged or ordered her.
We don't know if he'd rather have suffered
in their now forsaken German home . . . .

She smoothes the paste onto his arms,
his shoulders, neck, back, thighs . . . .
A future angel of the camps puts out our eyes.
It may be he grunts with pleasure, or fear,

or is it just to try to thank her?
A future angel of the camps puts out our eyes.

Life

The dreaded ones arrived. They did not know what they'd be,
       but did come to be.

They called themselves "Insanity" & "Angel." They had no color, no life
       left in them except

for how they candled themselves as though their perpetrator,
       if that is what he was,

had aborted them. No, but as though they were their own afterbirth
       after several decades

of remembrance, astonishment that such had happened, & terror. They had
       no color in them,

& their fat supposedly soothed papa who might have been better off
       if he'd not

been born into such as whatever was his story. They did have, shadowing them,
       a Reich whose mother

delivered children & then killed them for the fatherland. But they had no color,
       no life left in them.

Art

To approximate a mass grave,
I bulldozed mud, bonemeal, maggots
into a viscous conglomerate,

then into a glass box
the size of a cattlecar.
I piped in classical music—

Beethoven, Brahms, Wagner—
& authentic recordings of trains
clacking on murderers' tracks.

I bought my mud in Poland,
stained glass in France,
found bonemeal in Deutschland,

buckets of maggots by chance
when I dug beneath an altar
into a cess of flesh, & hair,

& scripture. So far, so good,
but my work seemed too stark—
this inspired me to wire

three black lightbulbs to be switched
on or off
as with a work of art:

the first to illuminate its roof,
the second its lowest layers,
the third its sacred heart.

Notes

The Swastika Poems

"Dutchman" ("A Snapshot of My Father, 1928") was a term used by Americans to label all those immigrants, including Germans, who sounded as though they spoke Dutch.

Earlier versions of "For Hermann Heyen" and "For Wilhelm Heyen" first appeared in my first book, *Depth of Field* (LSU Press, 1970).

Much of "Men in History" is based on Albert Speer's memoir *Inside the Third Reich* (1970).

I wrote "Passover: The Injections" after reading Susan Fromberg Schaeffer's powerful and moving novel *Anya* (1974).

"Darkness": Lev Bezymenski's *The Death of Adolf Hitler* (1968) describes the autopsies performed on charred bodies dug up by the Russians from the Chancellery garden. In *Adolf Hitler* (1973), Colin Cross argues that the Russian findings, particularly in regard to the body supposed to be Hitler's, are disputable.... When I first published this poem as a chapbook in 1976, I wrote a note to accompany it, an apology:

> *I remember that "Darkness" was an evening's outpouring. For seven or eight years I'd been reading about WWII and the Holocaust with a constant sense of disbelief, shaking my head as I read, thinking that all of this could not have happened. All my reading experiences, all of those walks through German cities and woods during 1971–2 when I spent a year there where it all began, a day at Belsen I'll never forget—I am there now as I write, the Erika over the mass graves beginning to pulse with spring—all these things led to the voice of fragment and obsession that is "Darkness." That same evening, just before the poem, in effect, wrote itself, I had seen the film* The Man in the Glass Booth, *its strange psychological leaps, and had walked home in a moonless darkness, my mind whirling.*
>
> *I am worried about the poem. What does it do? Where does it go? The speaker (the self I was, the selves, as I wrote) begins with the fear that he will lose the camps, forget them. But his words turn to say that it is not just that he is afraid he will not be able to hold the victims in his memory: it seems to me that he is afraid that he will miss the drama and excitement of that whole history. From this point on, there is no mental censorship of what happens as the speaker talks, as he projects his body into the bunker, as he imagines a grotesque and even perverse exhumation of his Fuhrer. (I hear, now, in some lines, my remembrance of the Russian autopsy report on that body dug up in the*

Chancellery garden.) The poem is haunted with cattlecars and skin lampshades. Within a book, finished, that will be called The Swastika Poems, *it says, if anything, something much of the book tries to articulate. It says* now, *says that this is all with us now, all these impulses, this sensibility, moral and murderous and sexual at the same time . . . .*

The epigraph from Peter Weiss for "Erika" is from "My Place," an essay about a day he spent at Auschwitz (*German Writing Today,* ed. Christopher Middleton, 1967).

"Blue": The quotation from Elie Wiesel is from *Night* (1960).

Sections II and IV of "A Visit to Belzec" are taken from Richard Grunberger's *Hitler's SS* (1972) . . . . It may be that because we as human beings, in ineffable and mysterious ways, share responsibility for the evils of history, a stance of moral superiority in poetry is often insufferable and always wrong. Perhaps the most *direct* damning takes place in two lines in this poem: "Curse them forever / in their black Valhalla" . . . . In a limited edition, *The Trains* (Worcester, MA." Metacom Press, 1981), I published the April 29, 1972 entry of a journal I kept in Germany that year. Now, more than forty years later, I want to quarrel with and correct and complicate my old self, but for the questions it raises, I repeat that journal entry here:

Worked at a poem last night. Don't know if it will come to anything. Haven't written a line since December, and I've learned: It can go away. It's easy to forget the concentration and awareness I used to snap into. I used to know what previous words and lines were doing and saying as I moved to the next line. But my brain is already going at different frequencies, and after just several months. Hard to explain. Since Belsen. Also, maybe that place knocked a lot of the fancy out of me, the relativistic dance. A moral poetry is so much out of favor that even the unconscious of American poets rebels against saying that men can be more than animals, that civilization means the recognition and control of certain instincts, that there is a divine moral order, that it is the psychotic who looks forward to destruction and genocide to complement his own psychosis, that man is an ongoing experiment in whom God is interested, that we must not give up to weariness and Weltschmerz and nihilism, that "moral" works of art can actually help to build a consensus for moral action. This kind of simplicity, too, will be twisted by the fashionable. Lord, help me to rid myself of the desire to kill other people, for my spirit wants to declare that desire alien.

I do not know how—are there other than slippery and ambiguous modern models?—to write that kind of poem, or am afraid to write it. But I have the feeling that most of the American "poets" of my generation are just fooling around, that we are indulging ourselves, throwing off thin and misty and evasive things, giving up to a vapid surrealism, telling ourselves that our foolish poems are really serious, dancing around the edges of amorality, declaring that we cannot communicate with one another, that all is lost, that this is the age of situational ethics and play. I have a feeling that one smell of the human smoke at Auschwitz would cure this . . . .

"The Numinous": The epigraph is from Otto's *The Idea of the Holy*, trans. by John W. Harvey (1958).

"The Uncertainty Principle": Willard Van Orman Quine is the author of *Word and Object* (1960), a study of the possibilities of precise communications through language. The quoted phrase suggests to me that our individual meanings for words are various and even eccentric enough to require constant and strenuous translation as we try to reach one another.

Erika

"Three Relations": Saul K. Padover was an American intelligence officer in psychological warfare who moved into Germany immediately behind our armies. Parts I and III of this poem follow stories related to him and reported in his *Experiment in Germany* (New York, 1946). The former is spoken by a German woman who had seen Hitler at Aachen, and the latter by a Frenchman who was forced to work at Sachsenhausen in 1944. Part II of my poem is based on passages in *The Beasts of the Earth*, by Georg M. Karst (pseud.), trans. by Emil Lengyel (1942).

"A New Bible": The epigraph from Primo Levi is from his *If This Is Man* (1959) . . . . It was at Treblinka where a clock whose hands pointed to three was painted on a false wall at the arrival "station."

"The Car": Hitler's fantasy is mentioned in *Treblinka*, by Jean-Francois Steiner (1967).

"The Hair: Jacob Korman's Story": This poem is based on an experience related by one of the survivors in the study by Dorothy Rabinowitz, *New Lives: Survivors of the Holocaust Living in America* (1976).

"The Funnel: Speech to Jews at Treblinka by Kurt Franz": Commandant Franz' speech is also reported in Steiner's *Treblinka*. The speech is insane, surely, and my parodical form is disgraceful, obscene. I realize that this is a dimension of several poems in *Erika*, presentation itself as obscenity.

"Dark in the Reich of the Blond" : I wrote this poem after reading *The Third Reich of Dreams*, by Charlotte Beradt (1968).

"Kotov": I've been unable to locate again the book in which I found the history of Ivanovitch Kotov, but his story is a true one.

"Mandorla": A mandorla is an oval medieval painting, probably one from which, in this case, the likeness of Jesus has faded or been cut. Paul Celan, or the "*ich*" of the poem, begins "In der Mandel," associating the German word for almond (with its associations with arsenic) with his title. The more I hear this poem, the more haunting it becomes. The eighth line, for example, suggests the eternity of the Jewish people, their death in the camps, and their inability to become wise. The penultimate line may expand this into a kind of holocaust of ignorance for all humanity. The last line is filled with horror and beauty.... I'm indebted to "Manifestations of the Holocaust: Interpreting Paul Celan" by Jerry Glenn in *Books Abroad,* 46, 1 (Winter 1972), 25–30.

"Death Fugue": I'm familiar with translations of Celan's poem by Michael Hamburger, Christopher Middleton, Joachim Neugroschel, and John Felstiner. While many of my words must of necessity be theirs, I've brought into my translation emphases and rhythms different from theirs that I feel in the original German.

"Poem Touching the Gestapo": The epigraphs are from Edward Crankshaw's *Gestapo* (1956), and Olga Lengyel's *Five Chimneys* (1972).

"The Halo": The story of Chicha is based on passages in *Fragments of Isabella: A Memoir of Auschwitz*, by Isabella Leitner (1978).

Falling from Heaven

"Children's Poem: This Village": Irving Greenberg mentions this village in his essay "Cloud of Smoke, Pillar of Fire: Judaism, Christianity, and Modernity after the Holocaust," in *Auschwitz: Beginning of a New Era? Reflections on the Holocaust*, ed. Eva Fleischner (1977).

"The Lice Boy of Belsen": Hanna Levy-Hass in her *Inside Belsen* (1982) tells of one such victim.

"Sonnet and Haiku: Forms from the Reich University": My poem is based on a letter quoted in *Remember Nuremberg*, by A. Poltorak and Y. Zaitsev (Moscow, n.d.).

"Scripture: Himmler on Mercilessness": I drew on the excerpt from Himmler's speech used by Jean-Francois Steiner as an epigraph to *Treblinka* (1968).

"Canada": For some reason unknown to me, "Canada" was the name given to a huge warehouse-dispensary-collection center at Auschwitz.

"Coin": I've taken the statistics in this poem from Irving Greenberg's essay (see note above to "Children's Poem: This Village").

"The Apple": The first part of this poem is based on an anecdote told to Helen Epstein in her *Children of the Holocaust: Conversations with Sons and Daughters of Survivors* (1979).

Shoah Train

"Roof": I found the poem's photograph in *Auschwitz: 1270 to the Present*, by Deborah Dwork and Robert Jan van Pelt (1969).

"Fugue for *Kristallnacht*": In memory of survivor Angie Suss-Paull (1922–2007) who allowed me to build this fugue which is based on exact phrases and sentences of hers that I wrote down as she was speaking to a class. In 2003 she included my poem in her *Angie's Story*, as told to Barbara G. Appelbaum and Peter Marchant, published by the Center for Holocaust Awareness and Information at the Jewish Community Federation of Greater Rochester, New York.

"Bloodhound": This Hitler outburst is reported in *Quest: Searching for Germany's Nazi Past*, by Ib Melchior and Frank Brandenburg (1990).

"Euthanasia Economy": I read of the Hadamar program and of the Munich killer-physician Pfanmüller in Klaus P. Fischer's *The History of an Obsession: German Judeophobia and the Holocaust* (1998).

"Milk Silhouette": Gerda Weissman Klein witnessed this murder. *All But My Life* (1957).

"Testimonies, 1946": One of our most powerful collections of survivors' testimonies is *Fresh Wounds: Early Narratives of Holocaust Survival*, edited by Donald L. Niewyk (1998). One hundred nine testimonies were recorded in Europe in 1946 by Russian-born American psychologist David P. Boder. Thirty-six appear in *Fresh Wounds*. For these ten fragments, I've stayed close to texts as found here, but Niewyk mentions extensive necessary "retranslation into more idiomatic English" for his versions to begin with, so I did not think it abusive if I cut a word or changed rhythms.

The general question of the editing of spoken testimonies is complex. Niewyk writes, "Boder insisted on a starkly literal, verbatim rendering of the original language, searching it for evidence of what he called 'deculturation' and various types of trauma. Here the objective is to let the survivors tell their stories as clearly and as intelligibly as possible, always in their own words, but with much redundant material excised . . . . Those for whom every hesitation, repetition, and convolution may be heavy with meaning ought to consult the original recordings or transcriptions." In fact, I'm one of those Niewyk seems almost to dismiss: I'd prefer a transcript that witnessed every repetition and stammer; I know, however, that such an undertaking isn't possible for me or practical for any publishing venture for anyone else—when only about one-third of the Boder interviews appear in *Fresh Wounds* to begin with—and Niewyk has labored strenuously and conscientiously to get to the facts and to make sure the survivors have their say. But I remember the moment when I heard Angie Suss-Paull say, "who will live / will die," as her unconscious omission of one or two words fused the death-in-life presence that so many survivors have tried to communicate to us. Any revision on my part toward "clarity" and "intelligibility" would, I believe, diminish Suss-Paull's witness here. Deepest testimony may reside in and emanate from wildness and apparent incoherence. (My poem "The Secret" in *Falling from Heaven* turns on this question.)

In these ten poems, and in "Catbird" and "The Head" where testimony, also from *Fresh Wounds*, is woven in, I am another listener with Boder and Niewyk as witnesses attempt to speak the unspeakable. Someday, maybe (to echo poet William Stafford), but probably not, each of the one hundred nine will have his or her own book with a recording of the interview itself, a verbatim transcription, and a translation with extensive notes. And maybe we can learn their full names. But even then . . .

"Parity": Primo Levi mentions this soccer game in *The Drowned and the Saved* (1988).

"Perpetrator": The story of the drowned child is part of the testimony of survivor and witness Joly Z. In his *Preempting the Holocaust* (1998), Lawrence L. Langer mentions this incident and discusses "the paradox of the disappearing criminal."

"Child": Langer (see above) mentions this Kovno ghetto incident. It is from Tape T-662, testimony of Charles A., Fortunoff Video Archive for Holocaust Testimonies at Yale University.

"Stones: The Efficacy of Poetry," "Ardor," and "Bread": I wrote these poems while reading *Auschwitz: A Doctor's Eyewitness Account*, by Dr. Miklos Nyiszli (1993 [first published in 1960]).

"Affliction": See *The Warsaw Diary of Adam Czerniakow*, edited by Raul Hilberg, Stanislaw Staron, and Joseph Kermisz (1979).

"Elegy": "Wooden Heart" may be found in Primo Levi's *Collected Poems* (1993), trans. by Ruth Feldman and Brian Swann.

"Revelation: Theresienstadt Story": Eva Roubickova's story may be found in her *We're Alive and Life Goes On: A Theresienstadt Diary* (1998).

"The Berries": I found the story within this poem in Raul Hilberg's *The Politics of Memory: The Journey of a Holocaust Historian* (1996).

"Star Song": Victor Klemperer mentions this dream in his *I Will Bear Witness: A Diary of the Nazi Years* (1998).

"The Presence of Absence": Charlotte Delbo related this incident to Lawrence L. Langer. See his introduction to her *Auschwitz and After*, trans. by Rosette C. Lamong (1995). At various points in this book Delbo says: "I'm living without being alive." "Presently, I am no longer alive." "I can't explain it any other way except by saying: I am not alive." "I'm not alive." "I just don't feel myself living." "I'm not alive. I died in Auschwitz but no one knows it." "Such is the despair of the powerless that grips me, the full awareness of the state of being dead."

"Candy": The epigraph is from Dawidowicz's *From that Place and Time: A Memoir 1938–1947* (1989).

"Visitors: Last Poem": In *Auschwitz: 1270 to the Present* (see note to "Roof" above), the authors discuss various controversial plans and designs for a memorial at Auschwitz-Birkenau. My poem draws heavily on a proposal made in the late 1950s by a group of Polish architects and sculptors led by Oskar and Zofia Hansen. "Their design," as Dwork and Van Pelt say, "refused to allow the ruins of the camp to become objects for others to arrogate."

A Poetics of Hiroshima

"It Came to Pass": my reference is to the last section of Robert Penn Warren's *Audubon: A Vision* where he requires of us, "In this century, and moment, of mania, / Tell me a story."

"Then: Ghost Story, 1944": I found this experience of Greek cousins Dario Gabbai and Morris Venezia in Laurence Rees' *Auschwitz: A New History* (2006). (See note for "Poetry," etc. below.)

"Museum Visitor Coda": In *The Politics of Memory* (see note to "The Berries" above) Raul Hilberg mentions that he proposed that the United State Holocaust

Memorial Museum in Washington devote a small room to this single can of *Zyklon-B* .... Writing this poem I somehow remembered the child I'd written of years earlier in "The Bear" in *Shoah Train,* and now hear her name.

"Lullaby": I found the story of the drowned newborn (which is part of the testimony of survivor and witness Joly Z .) in Lawrence L. Langer's *Preempting the Holocaust* (1998).

"Dr. Heim": What I know of Dr. Aribert Heim is also from *Preempting the Holocaust.* Langer's source is the Simon Wiesenthal Documentation Center, Vienna, *Bulletin of Information No. 34,* January 31, 1994, 3–4.

"Poetry," "The Word," "Exercise,": I found the central incidents in these poems in Rees (see above). Ernst Krankemann's actions ("Exercise") were witnessed by survivor Jerzy Bielecki and recorded in a BBC interview. Rees himself interviewed Wilfred von Oven ("The Word").

"Illumination Graft": In their *Auschwitz Report* (written in 1945, first published in English in 2006), Primo Levi and Leonardo DeBenedetti briefly describe the grafting experiments on humans done in Auschwitz, the first five lines here, and then the lighting in the operating room at Monowitz, the last four lines. In the poem's mind is the death of language, of concept, when life in the anti-world of the camps reverses everything so that compassion might mean killing someone, so-called food is sawdust, surgery is sadism, even *light*, which in the whole history of humankind has evoked evolution toward goodness and redemption and revelation, facilitates evil .... In *The Edge of Modernism: American Poetry and the Traumatic Past* (2006) Walter Kaladjian writes: "After Auschwitz, however, fire and light no longer find their sources in the unconcealment of truth but in the demonic burning of the death-camp crematoria." See especially "The Killers" and "The Light" further on in *A Poetics of Hiroshima.*

"Autumn Rain, 1946": I've adapted certain details for this poem from those in Leonard Mosley's *The Reich Marshall* (1974).

"Iwo Dahlia": I'm indebted to Richard F. Newcombe's *Iwo Jima* (1965) for much in this poem.

"The Carriages": Wanda Szaynok and Edward Blotnicki witnessed this orderly removal of baby carriages from Auschwitz. Laurence Rees mentions this incident in his introduction to *Auschwitz: A New History* (see above).

"The Light": In *Perpetrators Victims Bystanders* (1992) Raul Hilberg mentions such a discussion that took place at Belzec in 1942.

The Candle: New Poems

"Testimony of Christa Schröder," "Interrogation," "Volcano: Testimony of Alfred Hartl," "Sonnet Ending in Trite Rhyme": I wrote these poems while reading Gita Sereny's *Albert Speer: His Battle with Truth* (1995).

"The Murderer," "Sport," "Hitler Street," "Nihilism Crematorium": I wrote these poems while reading *In the Shadow of Death: Living Outside the Gates of Mauthausen* (1990), by Gordon J. Horwitz.

"Absence," "Luger," "Sound," "Reminder": These poems derive from testimonies in Henry Greenspan's *On Listening to Holocaust Survivors: Recounting and Life History* (1998).

"Shekhinah" and "Of Covenant": I learned of diarist Yitskhok Rudashevski in David Patterson's *Along the Edge of Annihilation: The Collapse and Recovery of Life in the Holocaust Diary* (1999).

"Determination": The Lagerführer in this poem is mentioned in Laurence Rees's *Auschwitz: The Nazis & the "Final Solution"* (2005). Rees also quotes the letter I use in "Bayer Co. to the Auschwitz Authorities."

"Katyń, 1941: The Germans": A recently released prisoner described these scenes to Hélène Berr. *Journal*, trans. David Bellow (2008).

"The Arrival: Dagmar Ostermann": In *The Meeting: An Auschwitz Survivor Confronts an SS Physician* (2000), trans. from the German and annotated by Susan E. Cernyak-Spatz, survivor Ostermann mentions this arrival as she confronts Wilhelm Münch. She is also the survivor I refer to later in "The Candle".

"Axe" and "Kurt M. Regarding the Shofar" are adapted from testimonies in *Remember for Life* (2007), edited by Brad Hirschfield.

"Sonnet Ending in Trite Rhyme": Speer talks of Hitler's increasing ugliness in Gitta Sereny's *Albert Speer: His Battle with Truth* (1995).

"Poem": In *Painted in Words: A Memoir* (2001) Samuel Bak remembers a voice from the HKP labor camp near Vilna when he was a boy: "Germans, Germans, Germans. *Imokh Shemam.*" Bak translates the Yiddish phrase: "May their names be eradicated." Instantly after reading this, "Poem" (I'd thought of calling it "Shalom" or"Golem" or "Flame") came to me quickly, hatefully, a cathartic curse once and for all against all the vicious perpetrators of the Shoah. Then, seeing what I had, worrying it for several reasons including the statements regarding art and poetry, for example, at the end of the fifth stanza of "A Poetics of Hiroshima," I realized I couldn't let it stand as it was even if I'd mean it to be read as a sudden burst of understandable anger and hate but not as a credo. For better or worse, my solution has been to include my "~~Poem~~" but to strike most of it out, to allow it to exist as an anti-poem of twisted prayer, revenge, judgment.

Acknowledgments

Grateful acknowledgments to the editors of magazines that first published many of these poems and prose pieces: *America, American Poetry Review, The And Review, Artful Dodge, The Blue Jew Yorker, The Carleton Miscellany, Chautauqua, The Coffee House* (England), *Colorado Review, Crab Orchard Review, Cream City Review, English Record, Four Quarters, Great River Review, Harper's, Hotel Amerika, The Humanist, The Iowa Review, Jewish Quarterly* (England), *John Berryman Studies, Kenyon Review, Margie: The American Journal of Poetry, Michigan Quarterly Review, Mississippi Valley Review, Modern Poetry Studies, NEO* (Portugal), *The New Yorker, North Stone Review, The Ohio Review, Omphalos, The Ontario Review, Pembroke Magazine, Ploughshares, Poetry, Poetry East, Poetry Kanto* (Japan), *Prism: An Interdisciplinary Journal for Holocaust Educators, Quarterly Review of Literature, Rapport, River Teeth, The Seventh Quarry* (Swansea, Wales), *Shirim: A Jewish Poetry Journal, Skywriting, The Southern Review, Strivers' Row, Tar River Poets, The Texas Review, 2 Bridges Review, Williwaw, Wisconsin Review.*

"The Trench" was first published as a broadside (Derry, PA: Rook Press, 1976). "The Children" appeared as a chapbook, *The Children* (Knotting, Bedfordshire: Sceptre Press, 1979). "Kotov," "The Hair: Jacob Korman's Story, "Dark in the Reich of the Blond," and "My Holocaust Songs" first appeared in *My Holocaust Songs* (Concord, N.H.: William B. Ewert, 1980). "The Trains," "The Legacy," and "Poem Touching the Gestapo" first appeared in *The Trains* (Boston: Metacom Press, 1981). "*Kristallmusik*" first appeared as a broadside (Farmington, CT: Versetility Books, 1995). "Parity," "Candy," "The Bear," and "The Others" first appeared in *Peace, In Deed: Essays in Honor of Harry James Cargas*, edited by Zev Garber and Richard Libowitz (Atlanta: Scholars Press, 1998). Carol M. Rosen first published "Stones: The Efficacy of Poetry" in *The Holocaust Series* (Book XVIII, 2000). "Revelation: Theresienstadt Story" first appeared in *Food Poems*, edited by David Lee Garrison (Dayton, OH: Wright State University Press, 2003). "Beauty" (originally titled "Art"), "Art" (originally titled "Religion"), "Education," "Prayer," and "The Maggots Speak" were published as a limited edition, *Holocaust Suite*, by Clarence Wolfshohl at his El Grito del Lobo Press (Fulton, MO: 2013). Several poems in *The Candle* were published as bi-lingual broadsides by Stanley Barkan at his Cross-Cultural Communications (Merrick, NY: 2015). Some poems and prose pieces have been revised since magazine and/or book publication.

I'm grateful to the original publishers of *Depth of Field* (LSU Press: Baton Rouge, LA); *The Swastika Poems* and *Erika* (Vanguard Press: NY); *Falling From Heaven* and *Ribbons: The Gulf War* (Time Being Books: St. Louis, MO); *Shoah Train* and *A*

Poetics of Hiroshima (Etruscan Press: Wilkes-Barre, PA); *The Angel Voices* (Mayapple Press: Woodstock, NY); and *Hiroshima Suite* (Nine Point Publishing: Bridgton, ME) . . . Profound thanks to all those at Etruscan Press who brought *The Candle* into being.

A Note on the Author

William Heyen was born in Brooklyn, NY in 1940, and raised by German immigrant parents in Suffolk County. He holds a Ph.D from Ohio University, and an Honorary Doctorate of Humane Letters from SUNY where he is Professor of English/Poet in Residence Emeritus at the College at Brockport. A former Senior Fulbright Lecturer in American Literature in Germany, he has won NEA, Guggenheim, American Academy of Arts & Letters and other fellowships and awards. Among his books (which are listed at the front of this volume), *Noise in the Trees* was an ALA Notable Book, *Crazy Horse in Stillness* won the Small Press Book Award, *Shoah Train* was a finalist for the National Book Award, and *A Poetics of Hiroshima* was a selection of the Chautauqua Literary & Scientific Circle.

Books from Etruscan Press

Zarathustra Must Die | Dorian Alexander
The Disappearance of Seth | Kazim Ali
Drift Ice | Jennifer Atkinson
Crow Man | Tom Bailey
Coronology | Claire Bateman
What We Ask of Flesh | Remica L. Bingham
The Greatest Jewish-American Lover in Hungarian History | Michael Blumenthal
No Hurry | Michael Blumenthal
Choir of the Wells | Bruce Bond
Cinder | Bruce Bond
The Other Sky | Bruce Bond and Aron Wiesenfeld
Peal | Bruce Bond
Poems and Their Making: A Conversation | Moderated by Philip Brady
Crave: Sojourn of a Hungry Soul | Laurie Jean Cannady
Toucans in the Arctic | Scott Coffel
Body of a Dancer | Renée E. D'Aoust
Scything Grace | Sean Thomas Dougherty
Surrendering Oz | Bonnie Friedman
Nahoonkara | Peter Grandbois
The Confessions of Doc Williams & Other Poems | William Heyen
The Football Corporations | William Heyen
A Poetics of Hiroshima | William Heyen
Shoah Train | William Heyen
September 11, 2001: American Writers Respond | Edited by William Heyen
American Anger: An Evidentiary | H. L. Hix
As Easy As Lying | H. L. Hix
As Much As, If Not More Than | H. L. Hix
Chromatic | H. L. Hix
First Fire, Then Birds | H. L. Hix
God Bless | H. L. Hix
I'm Here to Learn to Dream in Your Language | H. L. Hix
Incident Light | H. L. Hix
Legible Heavens | H. L. Hix
Lines of Inquiry | H. L. Hix
Shadows of Houses | H. L. Hix

Etruscan Press is Proud of Support Received from

Wilkes University

Youngstown State University

The Ohio Arts Council

The Stephen & Jeryl Oristaglio Foundation

The Nathalie & James Andrews Foundation

The National Endowment for the Arts

The Ruth H. Beecher Foundation

The Bates-Manzano Fund

The New Mexico Community Foundation

Drs. Barbara Brothers & Gratia Murphy Fund

The Rayen Foundation

The Pella Corporation

WILKES UNIVERSITY

Youngstown
STATE UNIVERSITY

Ohio Arts Council
A STATE AGENCY
THAT SUPPORTS PUBLIC
PROGRAMS IN THE ARTS

NATIONAL
ENDOWMENT
FOR THE ARTS
A great nation
deserves great art.

Founded in 2001 with a generous grant from the Oristaglio Foundation, Etruscan Press is a nonprofit cooperative of poets and writers working to produce and promote books that nurture the dialogue among genres, achieve a distinctive voice, and reshape the literary and cultural histories of which we are a part.

etruscan press

www.etruscanpress.org

Etruscan Press books may be ordered from

Consortium Book Sales and Distribution
800.283.3572
www.cbsd.com

Etruscan Press is a 501(c)(3) nonprofit organization.
Contributions to Etruscan Press are tax deductible
as allowed under applicable law.
For more information, a prospectus,
or to order one of our titles,
contact us at books@etruscanpress.org.

CPSIA information can be obtained
at www.ICGtesting.com
Printed in the USA
BVOW03s0204260617
487777BV00003B/1/P